TOWARDS A
Symbolic Architecture
The Thematic House

Charles Jencks

with photographs by
Richard Bryant

RIZZOLI
NEW YORK

FRONTISPICII EXPLANATIO

Symbolic architecture takes time to build and must be consciously pursued. It takes a good client and a good architect – the former represented in the frontispiece by a forward-stepping man and the latter by a strong woman (a traditional symbol). Filarete said that if these two were to fall in love there might be born, nine months later, a good building. Here the symbol of the good building – a veiled face – is mixed with that of a growing tree because the client and architect must nurture the building and oversee its development. They must also exchange the symbolic programme – represented by the smile on the face – which binds them into an act of architecture. The resultant strong building, supported by male and female elements – London columns – is composed partly of masonry arches, voussoirs and keystones, partly of draped curtains, and partly of its germinating seed, the tree of life. Directing the situation is the watchful mind's eye – consciousness – although Nemesis, the visiting comet or star, always threatens. Thus one builds symbolic architecture by conscious planning, but not always exactly as one pleases. The fatto explains this, while on either side is the dedication to Lily and Johnny.

Front cover:
Face elevation, Thematic House, painting by Chris Moore.

Back cover:
Thematic House, view of INDIAN SUMMER. (Photo: Ianthe Ruthven)

Overleaf:
Thematic House, WINTER into SPRING. (Photo: Ianthe Ruthven)

First published in the United States of America in 1985 by
RIZZOLI INTERNATIONAL PUBLICATIONS, INC.
597 Fifth Avenue / New York 10017

Copyright © Charles Jencks and Maggie Keswick
All rights reserved
No part of this book may be reproduced in any
manner whatsoever without permission in writing from
Academy Editions 7 Holland Street London W8

Library of Congress Catalog Card Number: 85-43050
ISBN: 0 8478 0659 6

Printed and bound in Great Britain

Contents

Introduction

ARCHITECTURE, ACCORDING TO AN ANCIENT RUBRIC, is the imperfect art. Like opera, it necessarily brings together many other arts and activities, including business. It is a hybrid concern, a mongrel or macaronic affair. Indeed, its essential heterogeneity has been recognised since Vitruvius defined it in the first century BC as 'Commodity, Firmness and Delight' (*Utilitas, Firmitas, et Venustas*). These three ingredients have remained fundamental but, as I shall attempt to persuade the reader of this book, they must be supplemented by a fourth which is just as essential: the symbolic.

For too long, particularly in our century, the ideas which architecture can represent have been overlooked as extrinsic to the field, and building, like a narcissist obsessed by his own image, has concentrated on its supposed essence – the qualities of space, light and function. This oversight – some will call it suppression – is shared by other arts, particularly those under the persuasion of a Modernist doctrine which is often based on the pure expression of each art form. But it is just as much the result of a pervasive agnosticism. Society, or in the case of architecture, the client, no longer gives the clear symbolic and iconographic directions which used to be an implicit part of the building contract, and the art contract, for that matter. What can an architect do in this situation – fire the client, or choose to be born in a different century? This book offers another approach: the conscious reassertion of the symbolic programme, the idea that every client and architect should make up an iconographic contract as explicit as their economic one. This treatise will put forward that claim, not prove it to everyone's satisfaction.

The first chapter of the book contains two historical sketches cast as melancholic and uplifting parables about our situation. The first shows what is missing, the second what could be done. But the major part of the book concentrates on my own symbolic designs, in particular the Thematic House, a house in London designed according to several iconographic programmes. As the title of this book indicates, the work is *towards* a symbolic architecture, the first steps in a new tradition, or perhaps the revival of an old one. It is not the middle of the journey and certainly not the culmination. When compared with the symbolic *systems* of the past – such as the Gothic and the work of Antonio Gaudí – our efforts and those of other contemporary designers look rather partial. Then, there were elaborately worked-out and strongly held beliefs, and a host of trained

craftsmen to carry out ideas in detail. This is not the case today, when an architect will be happy to throw in a column and call the result a deeply meaningful reference to the golden age of Augustus. A few stuck-on astragals do not the Pantheon make. And an individual could not reconstitute a total symbolic system – even if he were Leonardo with a PhD in psycholinguistics.

Nonetheless, several of us in different countries, now grouped under the Post-Modern banner, have been making modest efforts towards a symbolic architecture. A few books have been written, one or two exhibitions held, and this year's version of the signifying building is marginally better than last year's. (Vitruvius did say that progress in architecture comes from emulation and competition.) The first recent stirrings of the subject were found in the late 1950s in Italy and Germany, and in Christian Norberg-Schulz's *Intentions in Architecture,* published in 1963. My first writings on 'Meaning in Architecture' and symbolism date back to 1966 with a collection of essays George Baird and I edited on the subject. Since the late 1960s, with the infusion of semiotics (the theory of signs) into the discussion, there has been more and more interest in all aspects of meaning and communication. My two next contributions were 'Rhetoric and Architecture' (1972) and *The Language of Post-Modern Architecture* (1977), both of which argued for a multivalent, or many-layered, symbolism. The ideal was an architecture which contained coherent meanings, from the private and everyday to the public and philosophical.

Our articles and books were picked up in America, and by the mid-1970s Robert Venturi, Charles Moore and Vincent Scully, as well as a few architects in New York, were debating the issues and publishing books of their own. There was at least one important exhibition, 'Signs and Symbols of American Life', put on by Robert Venturi, Denise Scott Brown and their office in 1976 – a beneficent show, except that it drew lessons from dissociated symbolic buildings rather than integrated ones: the commercial vernacular rather than the multivalent work such as Antonio Gaudí's that I was stressing. In spite of these differences, however, a minor tradition of symbolic design has grown since then, even if it is not distinguished by much building, or a single indisputable monument.

After almost twenty years of thinking about and designing around the subject, and of watching others' efforts, I have reached only one firm conclusion: one has to be very explicit about symbolic intentions, and that means writing iconographic programmes. For if the meanings, or stories, are not written down and examined, then they cannot be criticised and will not carry much weight with the craftsman, contractor, client, or even designer. They will tend to be those embarrassed or kitsch symbols that we have seen recently, the ephemera tacked onto the building at the last moment. One has to write symbolic programmes to make them literally credible, something more than an advertisement, or Venturi's 'decorated shed', or a split pediment announcing with satisfaction 'this is the front door'. One has to write them out while designing in order to integrate the construction and function with the symbolism – which Gaudí did, and the School of Venturi does not. And lastly, the meanings have to be written down in black and white to keep the designer honest, to keep him from cheating too much, or straying from the point – always a temptation in an

Opposite:
Thematic House, the ARCHITECTURAL LIBRARY.

aesthetic age which tends to genuflect in front of The Big Gesture. The architectural profession, like the art market, goes a little weak at the knees when given a Shock of the New (or, by now, the cattle-prod of the old formalism).

From the tone, size and range of this book, some readers will have trouble placing it neatly in a category – on the coffee table, kitchen table or high table. I hope it will be read as a combination of genres, enjoyed for its legible colour photographs, used as an example, if not recipe book, for symbolic design and understood as being meant to change the state of architecture, if only by a small amount. I don't expect large offices which turn out a billion dollars of work per year suddenly to heed my warnings and go more slowly as they ponder the interrelationship of heating systems and solar symbolism. My guess is that they will mass-produce yet more 'ornamentalism' to give their megabuildings yet more explosive force. Nor do I expect architects, craftsmen and artists to have a sudden *rapprochement* inspired by the new synergetic power of the symbolic programme – although that's what I argue could happen. The cool reader knows, as much as I do, that we live in a commercial, fast-track production system with few religious, social or metaphysical beliefs that amount to more than mere pieties; and this is not going to change quickly. And yet, and yet . . . there are very real limits to continual agnosticism and the economic imperative, and there are real counter-forces at work among artists, clients and architects. Among other things, boredom with the economically motivated environment has set in, and it wouldn't be the first time that 'aesthetic fatigue' – that powerful nineteenth-century engine – caused a change of heart. I would bet that in ten years symbolic design (of varying quality) will become an accepted way of proceeding, if for no better reason than that the fatigue with meaningless formalism will approach high speed – if boredom can gallop.

Despite my advocacy of writing symbolic programmes, I should strike a note of warning. Except in rare instances, in the discussion of the Thematic House, I do not quote from these programmes, but rather describe the results. To do both would be repetitious. Nor am I saying that the programmes must always be written prior to design, or by the designer alone: rather they should emerge from discussions between client, craftsman, artist and architect. The point of the programmes is that the people who make them and use the building should find them meaningful enough. And that can involve giving up their separate interests to collaborate towards something. That something should be worked out near the beginning of design, then developed and then written down. A major reason for this method is to give more force and character to architecture – as well as meaning. Our environment lacks character ultimately because some of the people who build it don't believe in much of anything, and thus, paradoxically, the *aesthetic* point of iconographic formulae is to give strength and conviction back to building. In the past, symbolic intentions spurred expressive form because the architect knew what meanings to express. In a democratic, agnostic society these meanings have to be rediscovered and explicitly formulated by architect and client, or else the form will be, literally, insignificant.

★   ★   ★

A work such as this has to acknowledge three different kinds of debt. For intellectual stimulation and the development of my ideas on meaning in architecture I am beholden to the writings of Erwin Panofsky, whose scholarship and interest in the subject have always been a prime example. I tried to get him to collaborate on our anthology *Meaning in Architecture*, but at that period in his life he said that he was too old to take on the 'new science' of semiotics. To George Baird, Christian Norberg-Schulz and Ernst Gombrich I also owe philosophical debts – or are they bills of intellect – for their writings and discussions on the role of structure, intentions and convention in conveying meaning.

Secondly to my wife and family I owe more than intellectual IOUs; that is, an apology for making them go through what is now seven years of symbolic design. The process wasn't always easy or quick and to my wife Maggie Keswick, who was involved as client and critic the whole time, I owe more than thanks. Thirdly to the architects, firms and craftsmen who have worked on these buildings, yet another kind of acknowledgement is due. For the Garagia Rotunda on Cape Cod, Cape Associates and Fred Young were enormously helpful in carrying out my designs. For the Elemental House in Los Angeles, Robert Yudell and his firm Moore Ruble Yudell were equally important in realising the finished building, particularly when I was away. Robert Yudell and John Ruble also helped in the design and Tina Beebe devised the colour scheme. And similarly for the Thematic House in London, Terry Farrell and his office played a great role in carrying things through. I've tried to sort out these credits more fully in the text and appendices, but a special word should be said here, too, about the role played by the craftsmen Steve Agombar and John Longhurst. They managed to construct what were at times impossible looking ideas.

Finally, to Helen Roe for her drawings, to Richard Bryant for his always accurate and beautiful photographs and to Andreas Papadakis and the staff at Academy Editions – in particular Vicky Chaitkin, Pamela Johnston and Tim Slade-Jones – I would like to express my deep gratitude for making this a delightful object to look at. Whether one likes the prose and ideas or not, is, I'm afraid, my fault.

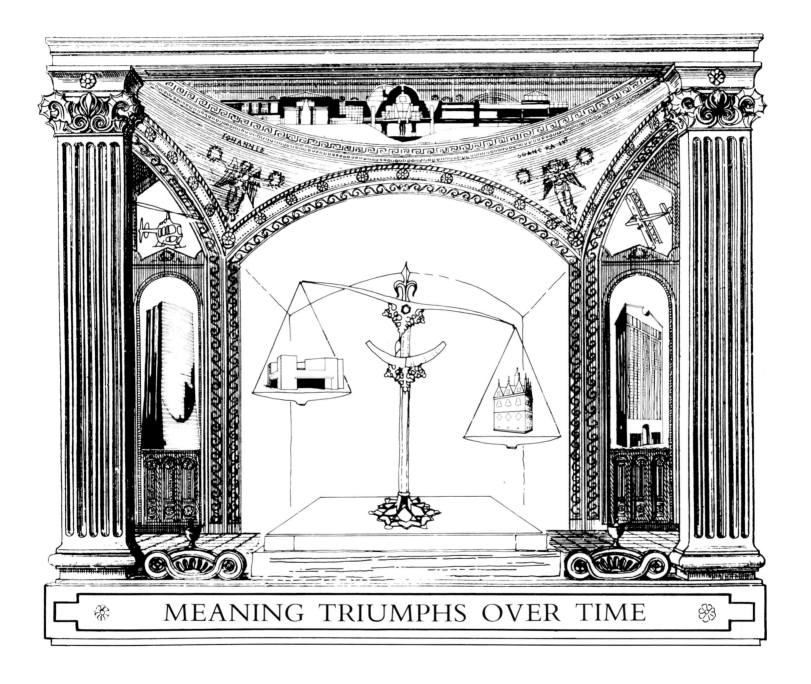

MEANING TRIUMPHS OVER TIME

CHAPTER I
Fables for Our Time
PART I

IMAGINE A COUNTRY IN WHICH A VERY STRONG DICTATOR abolishes religion, science and politics. The people of this country would continue to have beliefs and act privately on them, but as individuals increasingly expressed their discoveries in a language which no one shared, scientific truths would become a matter of opinion, religious practice would be limited to a few private revelations, and everyone would regard politics as about as interesting as filing their income tax. Soon nobody would believe anything of public importance and in all matters agnosticism would be the unofficial policy. Of course our dictator would have to compensate for this rather soporific atmosphere – even sex, food and gossip could begin to lose their flavour – and he might adopt the venerable methods of making the technology run on time and every public building beautiful, or at least striking. Efficiency and aesthetics would be the prescribed opiate of the masses in the land of Aesthesia. And it would not be too unlike the Brave New Worlds of science fiction, or the real pocket-dictatorships with which we have become familiar.

Emperor Bokassa, who ruled the Central African Empire like a wind-up Napoleon, characterises the type in every way but efficiency, with his extravagant self-coronations and ready-made symbols, the specially air-freighted Mercedes and Chateau Mouton-Rothschild '71. But Aesthesia would be more modest and industrial than this – a proper dictatorship. Instead of being clad in a thirty-nine foot ermine cape, our leader would adopt the style of his technicians and experts: the quiet grey mode of 'business as usual'. The people would make up for their public apathy by spending more time and money on their private lives. And although most collective meaning would have disappeared, one could still worship at the few monuments provided by the State. Like sports, these might still attract a large following, even devotion. On special holidays the Aesthesians would flock into the State museums and caress the stones, as they might have done the shrines of the past: the foot of the Statue of the Most Famous Beauty, like the bronze of St Peter in Rome, would be rubbed to a wafer-thin jewel. Our dictator would have a contented country and a relatively comfortable and docile public, secure with its ordered standards of private life.

Such a spectacle is familiar to us through literature, which people read because it represents a plausible future. Of course the Western democracies have not abolished politics – although they have made them part of the communications industry – and science and religion still have a minority of adherents, even if they don't greatly affect the public realm. But the total agnosticism of Aesthesia is too close to present reality for us to regard it entirely as fiction. This is not the Age of Cathedrals, or the nineteenth-century Age of Invention, or the Greek or Roman Republic, or even the Age of Merchant Adventure. The Space Age, to give it its most flattering name, believes in getting things done – in success – if it believes in anything. And you can't build monuments to pragmatism . . .

Or rather, we do. The dominant icons of our time are either public figures, who are noteworthy simply for being famous, or large corporations, which are often famous only for being big. Everyone who has watched television is well-acquainted with the former. To epitomise the latter, there is for example John Portman and Henry Ford's Renaissance Center in Detroit (1977), which is so big a Renaissance (at over a billion dollars) that it almost bankrupted the adjacent businesses and might have bankrupted itself had it not been too big to do so (1). Like Mexico or Brazil, which were also going under around the same time, it couldn't afford to go bust and was economically propped up. The symbolism of the architecture is quite powerful, even if unintended. Black 'glass stumps', to use a critical phrase put into circulation by Prince Charles, rise, if stumps can rise, like forbidding tombstones around a central cylinder of glistening black: a giant stack of plastic poker chips which signifies 'hitting the jackpot'. Or rather, as it has turned out, the empty pot. Clearly the building is as attractive to look at as it is reflective – especially from a great distance. One of the characteristic aesthetic tenets of Aesthesia is this: the further you get away from a megamonument, the better it looks. The optimum photographic point is one quarter of a mile, although some people will prefer several miles.

If the Renaissance Center inadvertently symbolises forbidding power and the Big Gamble, it also betrays the prevailing agnosticism through its blank facades. Where a temple or cathedral would have portrayed an idealised vision of the gods or a heavenly Jerusalem, these characterless towers portray a minimal content: no sculpture, painting or writing underlines the significance, because there isn't any. It's a fine Renaissance which has no room for art. Even the expression of architecture – the rhythms of the structural bays, the alternations of solid and void, the articulation of surface, the very poetry of past architecture – is kept to a minimum. Minimalist architecture, like the same movement in painting, is not just a celebration of a new technical beauty, but a good indication that the designer has nothing of public importance to say. At the Renaissance Center, it is limited to an announcement: 'Inside here there's a big empty space'.

It would be futile to go on saying more about less, or something about nothing, since probably most people have long ago settled down to the idea that they live and work in an agnostic society. What few are willing to admit, however, is that the agnosticism is so pervasive. One reason for this is that it is all so new and exciting to look at, so enjoyable, so well-serviced, and above all so sensual. The aesthetic pleasure to be derived from the Renaissance Center, or any of today's well-designed corporate headquarters, compensates for the missing content and makes us overlook the fundamental fact that such megabuildings are in functional and economic terms the cathedrals of our time, the objects on which we spend our 'surplus value', as well as a lot of time. They are really small cities in which, theoretically at least, one could be born, grow up, ride the see-through elevators, and die.

1 John Portman and Associates, Renaissance Center, Detroit, Michigan, 1977. Black gleaming slabs surround a black cylinder with floors stacked like poker chips. With Minimalist architecture, unintended associations are bound to arise.

2   Norman Foster, Hongkong Shanghai Bank, Hong Kong 1980-85. The expression of circulation, prefabrication and structure, the 'skin and bones', has taken an unusually large share of the budget. It is as if, lacking other parts of our body to decorate, we celebrated our blood stream and skeleton.

It isn't only the provocative pleasure of these creations which masks their emptiness; it is also their technical brilliance, and in this respect nothing is more advanced than Norman Foster's Hongkong Shanghai Bank (2). The masterpiece of perhaps the greatest High-Tech architect alive today, it is in many ways the *ne plus ultra* of technological architecture. Some of the largest spans ever incorporated into an office building are achieved here. And the office floors are suspended from bridge trusses above some of the largest, emptiest atria ever stacked one on top of another. Norman Foster has, effectively, divided his small city into a series of superincumbent villages, each with its own piazza-in-the-air. The price is not cheap, nor was it meant to be, as the Bank repeatedly insisted on having 'the best that money can buy'. Whether or not it is another billion-dollar building is a moot point, depending on how one does the calculations. However, the question is not so much the overall cost, as where the money has gone. Has it gone into the interiors where the bankers and public will understand and appreciate it? Has it gone into art to hang on the walls, or ornament and interior design which relate to the local culture? A good portion of the money spent on the architecture has gone into the structure and 'skin', as the cladding is known. That is, the Bank has spent a high proportion of its building budget on the wide spans and gleaming exoskeleton, and relatively little on providing a more comfortable, symbolically relevant interior. Foster has effectively redefined the artist as a technological craftsman and turned the whole building into a work of art, right down to the last lovely, movable, airplane floor panel. The premise that every functional element, from plug-in bathroom to exterior fire-stair, should be a striking aesthetic experience has used up most of the budget. And what do these mechanical elements symbolise? The equivalent of our muscles and digestive tracts, our circulation system and energy. The means of architecture have taken over from the ends, the part has been substituted for the whole.

No doubt the Hongkong Shanghai Bank building is the most potent symbol of corporate power and efficiency a Late-Modernist could make. Clearly it constitutes an investment in architectural technology which will be hard to beat, and the justifications put forward for it will resemble those for the Space Programme, even if in the end it proves to be not the Exocet of High-Tech, but rather its Concorde. And who is to say that Concorde will not ultimately prove to be of value, something more than an expensive executive toy? The extravagant inventions of one age often open the way for the democratic improvements of the next. The nagging question remains, however: what does all this investment *mean*, what does it *signify*? 'Doing more with less', as Buckminster Fuller said; 'Doing more with more', as the Concorde has so far proven; or perhaps, as Henry Adams long ago feared, 'We worship the dynamo rather than the Virgin'.

The answer is not entirely clear, and certainly not straightforward. When a Christian society starts to become secular then, as T. S. Eliot put it in a title of the 1930s, there is likely to be a pursuit 'After Strange Gods'. No single entity can occupy the place of a deity and there is bound to be a competing set of values among which the perennial ones – power, fame, money and energy – are only partial totems. The highest value in a secular society, both in spiritual and economic terms, probably resides in art, so it is to museums that we should turn to read the symbols of our time. Let I. M. Pei's widely acclaimed addition to the National Gallery of Art in

Washington D.C. stand as a symbol of these symbols. When it was finished in 1978 it was welcomed by 'extravagant press coverage – virtually all favourable' ‡. What does this building, placed in close juxtaposition with the nation's Capitol (3), tell us about the role of art today? Let us look first at the outside.

On its exterior, the East Building, as it is known, uses the same light-toned marble as the adjacent gallery and would be formally understated, like the surrounding buildings, were it not for its aggressive shape. In height, it keeps below the cornice line of the buildings opposite on Pennsylvania Avenue and takes its trapezoidal geometry from its irregular site. But this is where the public meaning stops and a host of private allusions start. Some of these pertain to the abstraction of Late-Modernism and its preference for Minimalist geometry rendered in a pristine material; others relate to precisionist construction – and no doubt this mechanical craftsmanship is admirable and appreciated. But then other associations rise up out of this inchoate form like the stereotypes inspired by a Rorschach blob. The main entrance is a giant dark slot, a cross between a gun-slit and that rectangular hole which swallows video-cassettes: the proportions are about right for the tapes. This emphatic void is contained in a flat H-shape, a veritable football post with elephantiasis, oriented for a 1,000-yard drop-kick at the nation's Capitol. These posts have funny skews with sharp points which attract the eye and hands of art lovers (but more about that later).

In front, where most museums might have sculpture, the architect has filled the space with an ice-field of jagged triangles which interrupt the main axis and make the visitor think of going down in the *Titanic*. This interpretation is reinforced by the fountain and waterfall which gush water down and down until it disappears mysteriously into an abyss hidden below another triangular skew. The fact that all these skewed ice-cubes are skylights over the cafeteria is, perhaps, an unintended metaphor of drink.

Once we have been sucked inside the cassette-mouth, the Minimalist language of solids and voids, of marbles and holes, continues to play on the triangular theme as if this were a paeon to the Trinity. One is confronted with a vast emptiness, yet another atrium exploded in scale like those of Foster and Portman, but here also reminiscent of a suburban shopping mall with nothing to buy and very little art to look at. Roughly forty per cent of the East Building is devoted to grand circulation and grand void, with the art treated as a peripheral matter. There is the standard giant red Calder mobile pointing in different directions – at the triangular maze of voids – as if it were an unsure traffic signal trying to make sense of this labyrinth (4). People rush off, clearly impressed by *le grand vide*, to be further aroused by the omnipresence of oblique and obtuse angles. These sharp corners – not dull 90° right angles, but 70°, 30°, and even 20° – jut out, come to a thin line and point. Razor blades of marble cut up the flowing space as if it were Emmenthal cheese. A 20° slice! How like the lifting prow of a ship, how like the swooping spire of a church, how positively . . . aesthetic! (5) The hand of the aspiring art pilgrim moves instinctively towards the marble razor blade and gently he caresses it. The miraculous corner joint: if God, as Thomas Aquinas said, is in the details, then He's certainly here in this knife of translucent marble. It has turned black with adulation and, like St Peter's toe, has begun to wear away (6).

Now in reality, this may well be a harmless piece of fetishism. But

3 I.M. Pei and Partners, National Gallery of Art East Building, Washington, D.C., 1978. A trapezoidal building on a trapezoidal site next to the Capitol building. Given its scale, lack of detail and huge H-posts, it looks like the base of some unfinished skyscraper. Only the material and height relate it to the surrounding buildings.

4 I.M. Pei and Partners, East Building, interior. A triangular space-frame above a triangular space that holds very little art. The architecture has triumphed over both the possible symbolism and the use of the building.

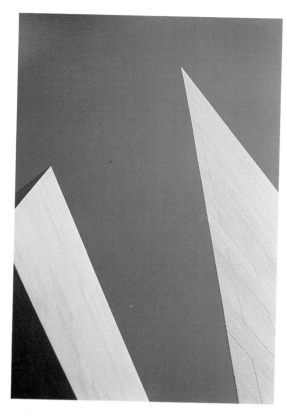

5 I.M. Pei and Partners, East Building. An exterior triangle of about 20° comes to a knife edge that cuts up the sky.

6 I.M. Pei and Partners, East Building, miraculous corner joint. People can't resist rubbing the blade.

Overleaf:
7 Pyramids of Chephren (foreground) and Mycerinus, Giza, Fourth Dynasty (c. 2500 BC). The pyramids are oriented foursquare to the Nile and the cardinal points. They are placed between vegetation and desert, life and death, and become gateways to eternity. They also represent the primeval mound that arose from the waters of chaos, and the sun's beneficent rays.

within our fantasy-land of Aesthesia we can read it as a grand cultural message. One role of the fetish is to substitute the part for the whole, *pars pro toto*, in this case the corner for the entire building. With a true fetish, the part takes over completely; a powerful case of this symbolic substitution can be illustrated by the instructive and sad case of the herring gull. According to the ethologist Tinbergen, a baby gull will peck at its mother's head, just beside the beak, in order to receive pieces of her well-digested food. This behaviour is instinctive and is triggered by appropriate signs – in this case the mother's colourful beak and the rings around her throat. Scientists have experimented with these signs and constructed an exaggerated wooden model of the relevant parts, larger in size and with stronger colouring. They show it to the baby chick, with what result? He would rather peck at the wooden model and die of starvation than peck at his real mother and eat. And, as if to get even with this unfilial behaviour, the mother, when presented with a worked-up version of her egg (in the shape of a brick, but bigger) would rather sit on this ersatz than on her own round one. In both cases, the fetish has so dominated behaviour that the birds have forgotten what the sign was for – an instructive point for our parable.

What is Aesthesia if not a land in which beautiful exaggerated signs distract the inhabitants from asking deeper questions – moral, spiritual and political? Overawed by the reflections in the mirrorplate, which they treat as a superior form of skin, fixating on the glitz like aspiring members of a rubber cult, they wander around in an aesthetic daze. Because they never connect one area of experience to another, their development remains arrested, focused for stimulation on the High-Tech structures that wrap around buildings as if they were in bondage. The environment begins to resemble S&M gear, reflective glass and the exposed truss replacing the rubber and chains. The continual and easy availability of such 'releasers', or supersigns (for that is what fetishes are) keeps the population happy but infantile. People are content with these substitutes, as our dictator knows.

Certainly, as with I.M. Pei's beautiful trapezoidal building, there is no social or religious significance to the shapes of Aesthesia. The forms may portray power and success, as in the Renaissance Center or the Hongkong Shanghai Bank, but have no deeper *raison d'être*. The moral lesson – and all parables must end with a maxim – is obvious. Before Aesthesia can become once again a land of signification, where parts relate to each other and to a greater totality, the notion of the underlying and unifying idea, or concept, must be reaffirmed. And this can be achieved only if the people who build the environment – client, architect, artist and craftsman – consciously agree on the substance of the shared meanings and on the language in which they are to be expressed. In order to avoid aestheticism, we must first agree on the content of the building or object, and in our pluralist society this means devising a conscious symbolic programme and affirming it as part of the legal contract. In Part II, we shall see a few exemplary buildings which related to this ideal in the past.

‡ See 'P. A. on Pei: Roundtable on a Trapezoid', *Progressive Architecture*, October 1978, pp. 49–59, where Dixon, Stephens and Filler, among other critics, give the building a rare if good-humoured scolding.

PART II

NOW IMAGINE ANOTHER WORLD IN WHICH EVERY thing has both a public and a private meaning. The leaders and the inhabitants of this world lead a charmed life because everything they do, no matter how insignificant, or even wicked, is part of some larger story. The great subconscious fear of mankind, both collectively and individually, that all action and belief are in vain is dispelled. Scientists, prophets and politicians, while disagreeing as usual about the fine print of existence, all see the point of the story of history: it has a shape in the past and a destiny in the future. The plot of the world's culture, though rich in variety, is still leading somewhere. And this direction, while it allows for different interpretations, is known and cherished by all. Everyday the inhabitants of Significatus – the land of meaning – awake like children amazed at the discovery of new relations between things. Their wonder is not dampened by complications – these are seen as further embellishments to the plot of existence, for everything, no matter how small or contradictory, has a role in the unfolding of the great chain of being. The Significatians have recently given up the old chore of jogging before breakfast and are thus happy to recite a tuneful simplification of the reigning philosophy: 'Egypt and China begin the story . . .'

This fabled realm is not so implausible. Almost all traditional cultures prior to 1800, while highly intolerant of each other, nonetheless had a strong notion of where they were going. It is an obvious fact, which would need restatement only in an agnostic society, that the great religions, and even the minor ideologies, gave history form – a beginning, a middle and, if not an end, then at least a destiny. The various cosmologies and social institutions filled out this picture, somewhat complicating it and even contradicting it in parts, but nonetheless relating to it. This web of signification also provided a basis for meaning in architecture that continued into the twentieth century with, for instance, the work of the Russian Constructivists. They, as part of the 'heroic period' of the Modern Movement, understood symbolism, although their followers lost their way. The Greeks, Romans and Christians (like the Moslems, Hindus and Buddhists) knew what to ask of their architects. Indeed it is only in our own era that the client has walked off the job and stopped supplying the symbolic intentions and style. Although our fabled land of Significatus may appear strange to us today, it was a norm in the pre-industrial past – a fact which becomes obvious with a look at the meanings of historic architecture.

The Egyptian pyramid is the most familiar symbol within this symbolic architecture (7). Four isosceles triangles rise up from a square base to provide both an image of stability and stability itself. Eternal permanence is the obvious signifier, understood directly from the heavy stone and shape. These perfect forms were meant to keep a Pharaoh and his culture alive for eternity. Hence the Pharaonic cult (which took place in the temple adjoining the pyramid) was tied to the cult of Re – the self-renewing sun god born again every morning from the east. The pyramid took on many precise meanings which all tied in with both daily life and cosmic time. Since the Nile runs south to north through the desert, it forms, as a geometric proposition, a basic axis of life set starkly within death. Every year it floods, inundating the parched land with fertile black mud. When the water recedes it reveals small mounds or islands of fertility raised up above the blackness. One creation myth describes the world being born out of the dark waters of chaos as a primeval hill. This idea of the primitive mound, worshipped as the *benben* stone at the centre of the sun cult at Heliopolis, is one possible origin and meaning for the pyramid. Very simply, it symbolises a powerful, fertile mountain – the primeval hill – from which springs life, often represented by the lotus and papyrus, as we shall see in the Egyptian column and ornament. But since a symbol is meant to mediate between everyday existence and eternity, it has several related meanings which unite the two.

One of these concerns the stepped pyramid, the ziggurat form which preceded the more perfect shape. This, according to Utterance 267 of the Pyramid Texts, was 'a stairway to heaven [which] shall be laid down for [the king] that he may ascend to heaven'. If the association of ideas thus tied the primeval mound to a stairway, it also related it to the sun's radiating light, or the cone of sunlight that falls to earth at an angle. Pliny the Elder said that the obelisk represented 'petrified rays of sunlight'. At the top of the obelisk, moreover, was a pyramidion, or tiny polished pyramid coloured yellow, gold or white. The limestone casing has been removed from most pyramids, but at Chephren's the remains of one can be seen (8). One can imagine that these glistening forms, set against the dark blue sky and sandy desert, must have appeared as dazzling images of the sun, especially when their brilliantly polished surfaces reflected it at the viewer directly. They became both a symbol of the sun god Re, and the place in which the king and his followers entered into permanent abode with him.

Another related meaning concerns the orientation of the pyramid to the sun's path and the axis of the Nile. Since the pyramid was placed on the West Bank and had its offering table on the riverside facing the morning sun and the fertile Nile, it became a very real gateway to eternity. The sun sets behind it and a thousand miles of desert, or death, stretch out *immediately* from this point. One cannot imagine this dramatic contrast from descriptions or photographs, and nowhere else in the world can it be felt as strongly. Superabundant life, then absolute death – the two meet in a physical line that extends more than six hundred miles to the north and south (9). The natural Cartesian axes are taken up in the square plan of the pyramid; the tomb chamber is sited facing west towards death, while the exterior temple dedicated to the cult of the king faces east. The king's statue, which holds his wandering spirit or *Ka*, is in a chamber or serdab facing the ever-present circumpolar stars, 'the imperishable ones' with which he wished to dwell. King Zoser, the virtual inventor of stone architecture, had his statue tilted back at the correct angle in his serdab to enable him eternally to view the North Star through two holes cut in the walls for his eyes. Here he sits, in what today looks rather like a space module, leaning back looking through his cosmic telescope. His foursquare stepped pyramid is oriented to the grid of the earth whose diverse elements he unites: Upper Egypt to the south; Lower Egypt to the north; the fertile part of the delta (life) to the east; and the desert (death) to the west. The sky rests on four pillars, the winds come from the 'four corners of the world' – it is as if everything can be understood and controlled by this perfect foursquare monument.

The Egyptian temple is also highly symbolic. Usually, there is a dramatic circulation path through it culminating in a dark, inner sanctuary where the shrine to the god is located. As in Zoser's stepped pyramid, this

8 Pyramid of Chephren, showing the remains of a limestone casing.

9 The Nile near Dendera. The sharp line between life and death – a green gash of life is surrounded for miles by sandy dryness.

horizontal progress can be conceptualised as a series of ascending boxes; the largest first – the exterior wall with the entrance pylons – followed by the open courtyard, and then by the enclosed hypostyle hall with its large, densely packed columns (10). Then, in a slightly raised, tighter space with only the dimmest of clerestory lighting, is the holy of holies. The dramatic passage to this is not unlike that through later temples – including Christian cathedrals – which it may have inspired. The purely architectural elements of space, light and material are given meaning and united to emphasise the social and religious significance. And as this is further underscored by painting, sculpture, reliefs and hieroglyphics, one can really speak of a formal *system* in the service of symbolism.

Take for instance the hypostyle hall of the Temple of Khnum in Esna. Khnum is one of the creator gods of nearby Elephantine, and is often represented as a man with a ram's head. At this particular temple, he is conceived as the creator of all beings, uniting Re of the suns and heavens, Shu of the air and Geb of the earth, as well as other personifications of everyday reality. He is also the guardian of the Nile, which ironically has deposited so much fertile earth here that parts of the temple are thirty feet underground. On part of the remaining hypostyle hall, his cult is combined with those of the Roman Pharaohs, who ruled Egypt from 180 BC to 251 AD. There are marvellous painted reliefs of their lithe bodies modelled by the raking sunlight. The Emperor Titus is shown being purified by the falcon-headed Horus the Elder, just in front of Menhyt, the lion-headed goddess who was

10   Temple of Khnum, Esna, 181 BC - 251 AD. The hypostyle hall survives with its open papyrus-form columns and relief carving which shows emperors undergoing initiation, or trouncing their enemies. The wall and column were both designed aesthetically *and* as places for symbolic description: in one sense *hieroglyphic* means *sacred sculpture*. Word, image and idea are one.

11   Temple of Khnum. The Emperor Titus is purified by Horus the Elder (left), and then is led by two women to the god Khnum (right). Titus' double crown is a composite of the head-dresses of the two women, and symbolises, like the papyrus and lotus decoration, the unification of Upper and Lower Egypt. Note the two plants tied together in front of Khnum – yet another symbol of unification.

12   A composite capital at Esna shows the papyrus and lotus intermixed. The polychromy gives the symbolism a rhythmical beauty.

13   The papyrus capitals swell out just above the symbolic rope-ties and then diminish to a primitive abacus, which carries the architecture. Some of the symbolism, a hieroglyphic, has been systematically chipped away.

14   Temple of Amenhotep III, Luxor, 1417 – 1379 BC. Papyrus stalks are bundled together, tied below the top, cut at both ends, loaded so that they swell, and then stylised in stone. Even the intercolumniation and entasis are designed – aesthetic refinements usually associated with the ancient Greeks.

Khnum's consort (11). Then he is shown being led by two women wearing the head-dresses of Upper and Lower Egypt, forms which are united in his double crown. These reliefs are positioned above shallow representations of the lotus and papyrus plants – further symbols of the two extreme ends of the long Nile. The plants grow out of the plinth, which symbolises, like the pyramid, the fertile earth, while giant versions of the papyrus – composite columns – hold up the entablature which represents the sky. Inside the temple this metaphor is made more explicit by the ceiling paintings of the heavenly bodies and divine birds. It is of interest that the papyrus column, invented 2,600 years previously as the first columnar order (12), is itself a symbol of the world arising from primeval waters. Its ideogram means 'to become green', 'to flourish', and the plants, when bundled together, signify triumph and joy. Thus the front of this hypostyle hall could be seen as a gigantic proclamation of triumphant rebirth. For those believing in the god Khnum, it was a sign of resurrection; for those believing in the yearly floods of fertility, it was a sign of the Nile and nature.

In a true symbolic architecture, the cosmos and the everyday are always united – a tradition the Egyptians continued over a 3,000-year period, making variations on a few basic themes. The three plant orders – papyrus, lotus and palm – are articulated in a variety of ways – open, closed and composite. The designer always kept one eye on the beauty and function of the column, and the other on symbolic realism: how the papyrus bundles were tied together at the top, how the stalks flared out under the weight and curved in to meet the ground (13,14). Thus one can always read the architecture as at once aesthetic, functional and symbolic – the fullest way possible.

How Egyptian architecture was transformed by the Greeks, Romans and Christians to meet their own symbolic systems is a story that has never been fully told, although the outlines of this history have been clear for some time. Rather than sketching this transformation, I would like to touch on an equally rich, but secular, counterpart – the Chinese garden. There are two reasons for this diversion: firstly the Chinese garden's rich complexity and spatial layering have influenced our design, and secondly the Chinese, like the Egyptians, have enjoyed a long, continuous development of symbolic design. Even today they aim to 'refresh the heart' as much by the meanings traditionally given to forms as by their sensual effect.

The Chinese approach to gardens has always been representational and allegorical. 'Bullet-hole rocks', 'moon doors' and 'vase windows' are some of the metaphors repeated so often they are almost like conventional words in a language (15). Sometimes metaphors which are too explicit are considered somewhat vulgar, such as the dragon-backed wall which undulates around a Shanghai garden. Others are more veiled, such as the same grey wall treated as if it were mist or even the background sky to a landscape scroll. One can place small plants and rocks against this 'scroll' so that they seem suddenly enlarged, like trees and mountains (16). Literally translated, the Chinese word for landscape, *shan shui*, means 'mountains and waters', hence rough rock piled up into mountains and little streams leading to reflecting pools form the basic structure of the garden (17). But their significance is greater than the simple mimicry of nature, for rocks and water are also physical expressions of *yang* and *yin*. Indeed, the whole approach to Chinese garden design can be read as a series of oppositions – high ground leading to low, dark spaces to light, enclosed to open – so the scholar can contemplate the principles of the universe within his own microcosm.

Against this general background are set very specific meanings. The garden was a place of dalliance, where lovers could play hide and seek among the rocks; it was a place where poets could show their skill and *littérateurs* name each part with an appropriate quote; a place where meanings accrued literally like barnacles – in the form of calligraphic inscriptions on stone. The greater the number of such tablets, the richer the garden.

The variety of meanings ascribed to just one element of the garden – the rocks – led to a form of petromania. Rocks shaped by the weather were valued as samples of mineral wealth as well as for their aesthetic qualities as 'nature's sculpture'. On a banal level, they were thought to resemble animals or monsters; on a more elevated plane, they were seen as frozen clouds, images of the eternal transformation of the *Tao* – that seamless web of time and change that encompasses all existence. So great did this mania become that the calligrapher Mi Fei was renowned for bowing every morning to the splendid standing stone in his garden which he addressed respectfully as 'Elder Brother'. Unusually shaped natural elements were thought to harbour nature's spirits, and thus it is not surprising that the Chinese immortals were believed to inhabit the rocky isles of the Eastern Sea. A pavilion set amongst garden rocks would thus suggest this 'Other World' and inevitably become a place of retreat from the court, or from official life. Indeed, some of the greatest gardens were built by famous drop-outs, gentleman-scholars who made an art of their exit.

The retired Chinese official has his counterpart in England in Sir Thomas Tresham. Knighted by Queen Elizabeth I in 1570, Tresham was

15 Yu Yuan, Shanghai, China. The Chinese word for 'vase', *ping*, sounds like the word for 'peace', so vase-shaped garden doors and windows constitute a visual pun suggesting the nature of the peaceful retreat within.

16 I Yuan, Shanghai, China, entrance courtyard. Shrubs and rocks are arranged in front of the white wall, which looks like the misty sky of a landscape scroll. The plaque above is inscribed with the name of the garden in antique script and, since the circle is a sign of perfection and heaven, the 'moon door' implies the association of the garden with the magical habitations of the Chinese immortals.

17 Wang Shih Yuan, Suzhou, China. In pavilions set among rocks (*yang*) and water (*yin*), enclosed in a labyrinth of interlocking courtyards, the Chinese gentleman-scholar used his retirement to cultivate himself through the contemplation of nature miniaturised all around him and the practice of the arts. Poems celebrating the garden's particular delights were engraved on stone in the writers' own calligraphy and, over the years, have added a depth of historical association to the enjoyment of the garden.

18 Thomas Tresham, Triangular Lodge, Rushton, 1595. The south-west 'salvation' side (left), has the inscription 'I have considered Thy works, O Lord, and been afraid'. Within the gable on the left is a dove upon a serpent coiled about a globe, while within the one on the right is a hand placed over the sun, the Pentecostal fire.

converted to Catholicism in 1580 by a convincing Jesuit missionary. He then spent the next thirteen years in prison for his new beliefs – time well spent for the cause of symbolic architecture. There he planned, as intricate geometrical propositions, several buildings for his estate in Northamptonshire. Among those finished is the Triangular Lodge, his answer to the triangular pyramid, but dedicated neither to the sun god Re nor, like I. M. Pei's East Building, to a left-over trapezoidal site, but to the Trinity.

Everything in this small building spells out the treasonable message of the High Mass and the Trinity (18). The structure has three storeys surmounted by three gables; its three sides are each thirty-three feet long. The windows are built from trefoils, as is the doorway (19) with its inscription *Tres testimonium dant* ('There are three that bear witness'). *Tres* is of course the Latin for three, but also a pun on the owner's name, a conceit common among the Elizabethans, and again today among the Post-Modernists. Even the metal tie bars take up the 'TT' and thus become a double pun on Thomas Tresham and the Trinity. At the top of the central chimney is a *Tau* ('T') cross within a chalice enclosed by a pentagon, which usually symbolises salvation, a meaning confirmed by the inclusion of the Latin word *salus*. Just below the gable cornice, on the south-west side, is the Latin inscription meaning 'I have considered Thy works, O Lord, and

19 Thomas Tresham, Triangular Lodge. The inscription over the door, 'There are three that bear witness', is also a pun on Tres-ham.

been afraid', while in the gables are further symbols of the third person of the Trinity: the dove perches upon a serpent coiled about the globe, and a hand is placed over the sun, the Pentecostal fire. Just above these two emblems – in triangular pediments, where symbols are conventionally placed – are the dates of Tresham's conversion (1580), and release (1593). Thus again the symbolic building mediates between the personal and the public, the transitory and the eternal.

Once we discover a symbolic system, we inevitably look for more meanings to confirm the plot or even, *per contra*, for mistakes or cheating by the designer. This is an obvious part of the fun. Why did Tresham allow himself a cross, on the lower windows, surrounded by *four* small round windows? (20) Clearly the cross is acceptably Christian, but the four windows seem rather permissive. It is only after we've counted in the smaller round windows (to make twelve) and then looked closely at the details that we understand his ingenuity in winning the game just when we thought we had him beat: the twelve apostles are perhaps signified, but also the sacred number *three* times four. We should really be counting the round windows three to a side, not, as we misperceive them, four, as can be seen by the way the set of three inflect towards the centre. This minor discovery, unimportant in itself, is typical of our reading of symbolic architecture in general, for wherever the mind finds a system of meaning it is led on to seek, and thereby discover, more.

Detective work, or playing the game of 'Hunt the Symbol', is one of the great pleasures of looking at symbolic architecture – as has recently become the case with Dutch genre painting. One has to know something of the language and conventions, but this takes a minimum of effort and, once learned, leads in all sorts of unexpected directions. There is an enclosed garden, the Pleasance, in Scotland – produced around the same time as Tresham's Triangular Lodge – which illustrates this point. Sir David Lindsay built his symbolic garden at Edzell Castle (21), as an illustration of his aspirations. On three sides it has relief panels representing the personal qualities he desired (the Seven Cardinal Virtues), which were to be strengthened by good education (the Seven Liberal Arts) and watched over by good fortune (the Seven Planetary Deities). We enter through a low door showing the Lindsay coat of arms with Sir David's proud motto *Dum Spiro Spero* ('While I breathe I hope'), which is taken up also in the low, box topiary (22).

As we look at the chequered pattern of these arms, and then at the wall, we begin to understand that the architectural pattern – three rows of voids arranged chequerwise – is a repetition of the pattern of the arms. Once we perceive this connection, we look for others . . . and find them. The heraldic colours are repeated in the planting – white and yellow flowers for *argent*, with blue paint in the voids for *azure* (the colour has faded). The last colour, *gules* or red, is obviously in the dark, local sandstone of the castle and the garden wall. Birds fly into their nests in the voided stars borrowed from the Lindsay crest (23). Accompanied by his personifications of Jupiter, Rhetoric and Prudence, Sir David has thus created a personal microcosm in the midst of the open Scottish farmland.

Symbolic architecture has fared well at different times since the Renaissance, especially during periods of revolutionary or artistic change such as the late eighteenth and late nineteenth centuries. On a popular level it

20 Thomas Tresham, Triangular Lodge. The foursquare window is in fact another symbol of the Trinity.

21 Sir David Lindsay *et al.*, The Pleasance, Edzell Castle, Scotland, 1604. The alternation of niches and chequers on three sides carry personifications and emblems of the Seven Cardinal Virtues, Seven Liberal Arts and Seven Planetary Deities – all meant to increase the *virtù* of the owner, whose motto *Dum Spiro Spero* even appears in topiary.

22 Sir David Lindsay, The Pleasance, with the Lindsay coat of arms over the low entrance. The busts in the niches and the dividing pilasters have been removed.

23 Sir David Lindsay, The Pleasance. The flower boxes have the *fes chequy argent* – the silver or white of the arms, while the *gules* is symbolised in the red garden wall. Note the seven ray mullets or stars, also part of the Lindsay crest, which centre on a hole for birds' nests!

has always played a part when people have built their own houses, or constructed and planted their own gardens. Eighteenth-century French theorists such as Boffrand and Blondel proposed an approach to symbolism which culminated in the *architecture parlante* of Ledoux, Boullée and Lequeu with their often fanciful and sometimes 'beautifully ugly' symbolic design. Somewhat later, there was a British counterpart to this; the associational theories of Archibald Alison and J. C. Loudon which influenced the work of Sir John Soane, William Burges, Norman Shaw and Charles Rennie Mackintosh. About the turn of this century, with Art Nouveau and its related modes, there was an explosion of symbolic design throughout Europe and America. Antonio Gaudí was clearly the master of this genre, but it included on the continent the work of Victor Horta, Hector Guimard, Otto Wagner, Josef Hoffmann, Joseph Maria Olbrich, Peter Behrens, Hendrik Petras Berlage and Michel de Klerk; in America some of the work of Louis Sullivan and Frank Lloyd Wright; in England that of William Lethaby, Charles Harrison Townsend, C. F. A. Voysey, M. H. Baillie Scott, and at times Sir Edwin Lutyens and numerous Arts and Crafts architects. None of these architects was completely committed to a symbolic architecture, but all of them at one time or another combined aspects of this with their new aesthetic manner. Perhaps the impetus to reinvent the architectural language always includes both visual and semantic components. The work of Charles Rennie Mackintosh is typical in this respect.

Mackintosh was always searching for an old/new dialect of architecture suitable for his Scottish setting – 'as indigenous to our culture as wildflowers'. In several papers between 1891 and 1893, he defined this new 'indigenous' architecture as having 'purpose', 'content' and 'a code of symbols' – ideas which he undoubtedly took in part from Lethaby, whose *Architecture, Mysticism and Myth* had appeared in 1892. We can see the realisation of these aims in several of his buildings, notably the Willow Tea-Rooms of 1904.

The Room de Luxe is, as its hybrid name suggests, a haunting and beautiful transformation of English and French ideas, all of which are directed towards the metaphor of the willow tree, which furnishes the basis for the symbolic programme followed throughout the building (24). The tea-rooms are in a street in Glasgow called Sauchiehall, which means 'alley of willows', and Mackintosh and his wife Margaret Macdonald took a poem by Dante Gabriel Rossetti as their point of departure for an effective stylisation of the tree. The opening lines convey an elegant sadness and mysterious whiteness echoed in the design:

> 'O ye, all ye that walk in Willowwood
> That walk with hollow faces burning white. . .'

There is something slightly melancholic about the design, epitomised by Margaret Macdonald's centrepiece, a gesso panel of women wandering under willows as if under some spell of nature – explaining, perhaps, why London critics derided the Glasgow Four as the 'Spook School'. The critics failed to appreciate, however, that the work is intended to convey a variety of meanings and moods (25). The Room de Luxe manages to be both a sparkling French hall of mirrors and an intimate place for tea. The room is scaled down by its basic division into white curved ceiling and reflective wall, with a dado level 3'9" from the floor. The leaded windows, with their abstract representation of the willow tree, also convey, by means of the

24 Charles Rennie Mackintosh, Willow Tea-Rooms, Sauchiehall Street, Glasgow, 1904. The street name means 'alley of willows', one inspiration for the symbolic programme that was carried throughout the interior and hinted at on the exterior, in the thin white mullions.

25 Charles Rennie Mackintosh, Willow Tea-Rooms. The Room de Luxe, the heart of the scheme, had a forest of tree trunks abstracted as mullions and chairbacks, while the chandelier and painting suggested hanging willow branches. (Contemporary photograph)

26 Charles Rennie Mackintosh, Willow Tea-Rooms, detail of the willow patterns and mirrors reflecting the windows, which are a transformation of the same idea.

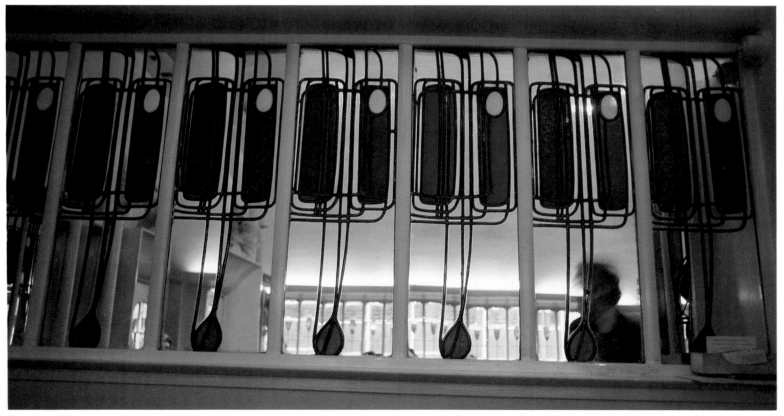

shimmering white fillets which divide them, the idea of a forest of white trunks (26). The original high chairbacks and the jewel-like doorway with its stylisation of a diminishing trunk also picked up this theme. And the original crystal chandelier, not restored, was a shower of abstracted willow leaves. Blue willow pattern crockery and the predominate motif of a flat, pinnate willow leaf further emphasise the central theme.

Such small and insignificant building tasks as a tea-room show how far we have travelled from Chephren's pyramid. We live in an age in which, it appears, boutiques and World Fairs have taken the place of the temple and town hall, at least when it comes to symbolic expression. Secular building tasks dominate – and they don't ordinarily inspire or sanction public expense on architecture. However much we love the telephone service and its profits, it nonetheless seems a bit ridiculous to build a monument to the AT&T corporation that focuses – as it does it New York City – on a gilded statue of the Genius of Electricity (27). The content of the symbolism matters as much as the form, and unless people find the content credible it becomes a form of camp or kitsch. What are we to do in an agnostic society in which people find no subject of compelling interest?

Five major areas remain from which to derive a significant content: traditional social use or the function of the building type, literature, religion, scientific discoveries which inspire wonder, and personal history. Each one of these areas may become the pretext for a symbolic programme, story or scenario. The design may start with a small or modest subject, such as the Lindsay coat of arms, which is then generalised to epic proportion, or at least to become a whole garden. Conversely it may start with a grand idea, or *concetto*, such as the Trinity at Tresham's Triangular Lodge, which is then focused down on the individual. Despite the fact that our epoch has no goal, nor even an overriding aim as had the Renaissance, it *is* a period of many simultaneous directions, of pluralism. And this, coupled with the widening of our detailed knowledge, means that there are more experts to consult on every possible subject – assuming one has a subject in mind. In the design of the Thematic House, we took advantage of this by asking, for instance, cosmologists and scientists for advice on how to represent aspects of the universe; characteristically they offered to help for the pleasure of participating. And here we touch on a surprising aspect of our time; despite the reigning abstraction and agnosticism, there is an untapped desire among several artists for an iconographic programme – to be able to paint, sculpt, draw and decorate an idea they find credible and can participate in shaping. And on the part of scientists, art historians, MPs, poets and astronomers, there is an unexploited desire to be able to share discoveries and values with artists so that they become a subject of expression.

One of the advantages of symbolic design over abstraction or merely aesthetic or functional architecture is that it adds something to the motivation behind both the making and perceiving of the work. It offers the artist the challenge of reaching beyond his own solutions in ways he hasn't foreseen. Admittedly, it may also result in a regression to stereotypes of the past, but this happens with Modern art as well. When there is, however, a creative combination of artist and symbolic programme, the result is a synthesis which extends the meanings of the art, and not just to a wider audience. Such a combination fundamentally deepens the seriousness and integrity of the work itself.

27 Johnson/Burgee Architects, AT&T Building, New York City, 1978-83. No doubt the space needed some focus, but the ironic sacrilege shows both the desire for symbolism and the lack of belief in it.

28 Lluís Domènech i Montaner, Palau de la Musica Catalana, Barcelona, 1905-08. Busts of Palestrina, Bach and Beethoven above stone columns, and a sculpture group by Miguel Blay at the corner, unify both sides, as do the interwoven arches.

29 Lluís Domènech i Montaner, Palau de la Musica Catalana, archway contrasting local composers with Wagner; in the background are the Muses of music in stone and ceramic, playing and singing as their followers do on the stage.

30 Lluís Domènech i Montaner, Palau de la Musica Catalana, the central skylight hangs down in a curious, 'burning' inverted dome, both a sunburst and transformation of the structural side fan vaults.

Finally, the justification for symbolic design lies in enjoyment. It is a property of the human mind to seek meaning, both on a trivial and a profound level. Our eye and hand, our ear and nose, are all attuned to the nuance of signification: perception is never pure feeling, but, as psychologists and wine-tasters remind us, an event directed by habit and hypothesis; what we know and care about. If this is true of the nervous system, it is even more so of the mind. We read everything we see for its significance and are frustrated when our environment does not fit together and reward our expectation that life is meaningful. Man has been defined as the animal that seeks meaning – that turns a Rorschach blob into a face, or senseless entropy into a morality tale. This is of course as true of Modern architects as of anyone. I can remember Walter Gropius, quoting Nietzche, say: 'Give a man a why to live and he can bear almost any how'. The problem has been, however, that the Modernists have not consciously pursued these 'whys' – the various plots, the local meanings, the conventional stories of society. Take the typical concert hall or theatre of our time – the Festival Hall in London or Lincoln Center in New York. Compare it with those of the past, even of the nineteenth and early twentieth century, such as the Paris Opéra, or Barcelona's Palau de la Musica Catalana with its representations of classical and popular music (28-30). Disregarding differences in style, the fundamental opposition between these pairs is between a building with only a minimal content and one with a symbolic programme. It is true that the Festival Hall was meant vaguely to recall ships, and the Lincoln Center to echo, however dimly, the Acropolis, but these associations are so minor, so lacking in credibility, that they were not written into the programme or considered as important as the function and cost. No one really believed strongly enough in the content, and this became a private matter, a bias of the designer smuggled furtively into the building.

But the situation is not as hopeless as this might suggest. In many ways we *do* inhabit the land of our parable, Significatus, because almost everything already does have some significance for someone. The problem is that the totality of these rather private meanings lacks coherence and purpose. There are divisions of taste, language, nationality and ideology which render any overriding system immediately suspicious, or literally in-credible. And this is a natural consequence of pluralist democracy and secularisation. Assuming this evolution of our culture is in some ways desirable, a greater burden than ever is placed on tradition and theory. History, or rather our many histories, can become one touchstone, with the high points and individuals in it used as standards – beacons for navigation and models against which to measure our efforts. The various Western and non-Western traditions are a repository both of events and ideas which can guide us and quickly show any imbalance of approach. And theory can emphasise the importance of explicit symbolism: if one point is clear from the study of history it is that such events as the Renaissance were not achieved by accident. Ideas, purpose, in short the *content* of art and of actions, motivated the protagonists of those charmed periods. Thus to compensate for the lack of focus in our pluralism, we must write down explicitly what we want our architecture and art to signify. To prevent it from becoming merely illustrative, or propagandist, this content must command assent and thus must be persuasive itself – that is relevant, perhaps even profound. Significant content is the *sine qua non* which guarantees nothing, but allows a deeper architecture to emerge.

CHAPTER II
First Steps Towards Symbolism: The Garagia Rotunda

Opposite:
1   The path through the woods twists several times, focuses on a seat which is a small version of the house, and finally turns towards the studio.

Above:
2   In China the scholar's *chai,* or retreat, was often a simple hut set in nature – or here a fantastic rock garden.

3   The view down the ridge focuses on a pond which is at right angles to the ocean.

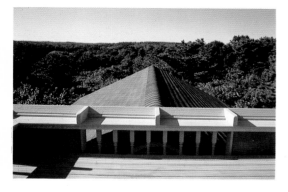

WHEN I STARTED WORK ON THE GARAGIA ROTUNDA in 1975, architecture was going through one of its recurrent periods of doubt. The very notion of architecture as an art, an elite profession, or a symbolic act of expression, had been criticised during the past ten years, and now Modernism itself was under attack. Designers were looking for a fresh approach that might grow out of, not contradict, the tradition they had inherited. At this time, I formulated the notion of Post-Modern architecture and began experimenting with several ideas. This studio is a result of these speculations: it tests the idea of mixing Classical and vernacular elements in a free way, using ornament symbolically and reintroducing the body image, or anthropomorphism, into building.

The studio is completely isolated in the woods. There are no roads, no electricity poles and, now, hardly even a path (1). I do not know of any other house quite like it, except perhaps in fables, for the obvious reason that such houses are hard to build and even harder to service: grocery delivery is impossible. But this house is just used as a studio – a retreat for work, for writing, or for drinking and listening to the breeze in the pine trees. If there is a building-type to which it relates (apart from, perhaps, the grandmother's house in *Little Red Riding Hood*), it is the traditional *chai* of the Chinese scholar, set within an idealised and undisturbed nature (2). Here the scholar worked, drank with friends and contemplated what was very often an artificial landscape. The scenery surrounding this Cape studio, however, is a very natural one of sand dunes, ponds, scrub pines, hog cranberry and oaks; these provide a dense green backdrop for what is the most remarkable aspect of Cape Cod – its clear, almost Grecian light. My wife, Maggie Keswick, who was writing a book on Chinese gardens at the time, was involved in choosing the exact site and orientation, so that the ponds could be seen – but not the neighbours (3).

Visitors to the Cape are always struck by the changes of blue – sky, ponds, ocean. In 1978, this inspired the New York photographer, Joel Meyerowitz, to produce a book, *Cape Light*, with such weirdly beautiful effects that sceptics accused him, quite falsely, of using filters. The light varies in its tone and sharpness and this, along with the landscape of sand dunes and blue ponds, has produced a school of Cape painters – originally led by Edward Hopper and Edwin Dickenson – who have captured a way of looking at the landscape that is characteristic of the sensibility of many of the Summer residents.

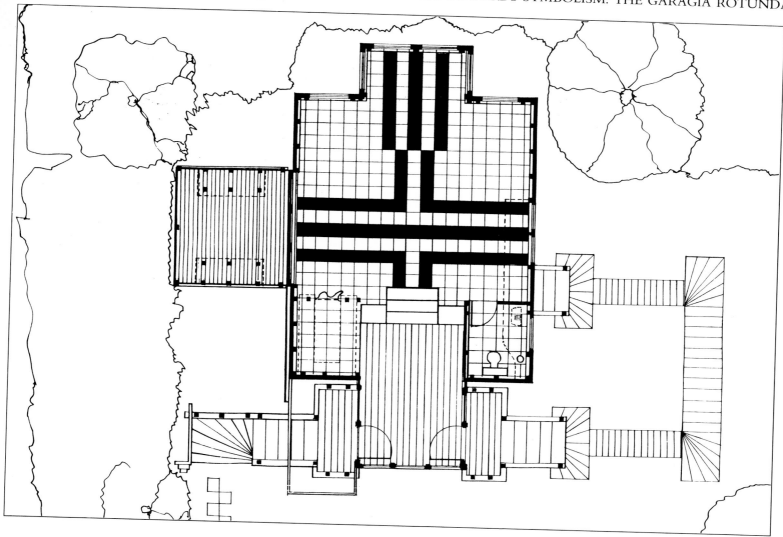

Opposite:
4   The blues of the frame reflect the variety of blues of the sky, sometimes even merging with them. Red is introduced only twice: here it marks the power supply. The pediments mark the door that actually works.

Above:
5   The plan shows the overlapping series of small spatial units organised on a meandering S-curve.

Overleaf:
6a, 6b   The frames of the door and rotunda extend into nature to emphasise the Classical opposition between the artificial building and the natural landscape.

It was the aspect of changing, purifying blues which I tried to represent in the ten shades which colour the frame of the studio (4). As one watches the gateway (or porch frame) throughout the day, the changing sky makes dark blues become light, the relative density of each switches place, and the lighter hues actually look darker than the dense ones, especially when they are in the shade. This can be quite extraordinary at times, particularly when a wooden post or beam suddenly disappears altogether into the blue background of the sky. At such moments as these, the sky is captured by the building and taken into its composition.

Every day, those who live in the woods by the ocean walk back and forth between pine-enclosed ponds (small lakes in reality) and a wide, sandy, open beach that runs thirty miles in each direction. During the Summer, the rare mixture of cold salty sea and warm freshwater lakes begins to build up an image of simplicity and restraint – though some may find it hard to grant in the middle of August, when there are two cocktail parties an evening. Nonetheless, the myth is still there. The ideas of retreat, informality, even purity – all sacred dicta of Rousseau's noble savage – are put into practice, at least before 5.30 in the afternoon.

The studio is a mixture of two different languages, as is characteristic of much Post-Modern architecture. The basic shell is based on a type of prefabricated garage (although it was finally hand-built) common in Cape Cod. The Shingle Style, the roof pitch and many of the elements, such as the garage door, are also common in the area and were therefore cheap and easy

Opposite:
7 Framed views of nature are possible in all directions. Note the circular shadow and the windows that view the ground.

8 The culmination of the route is the balcony set over bushes and a view of the pine trees.

Above:
9 The garage door opens to reveal another porch and vista.

Overleaf:
10, 11 The aedicule, with its permanently blowing curtain, is related to the chairs and table by means of its colours and proportions.

to obtain. But the Cape vernacular was also chosen because it is understood by the local inhabitants and builders (6). It is their language and – since I was away when the building was constructed – thankfully so. No supervision was needed, no working drawings, and the basic shell cost only $5,500. The idea of the vernacular, of being able to specify a building verbally or, as in Moholy-Nagy's dream, even order it over the telephone, was pursued with varying degrees of success. The most obvious failures, the mistakes and deviations from the rudimentary sketches, were decorated later. It was a Modern architect who said, disparagingly, 'Decoration always hides a fault in construction'. But so it should. Here, ornament – balusters, paint and a pelmet at the rear shaped like a face – covers the mistakes, while also working in symbolic ways.

In addition to the local vernacular, there is a superimposed language which is quite alien to the area and has more to do with the painted carpenter-built houses of San Francisco than the Cape. Queen Anne Revival, the elaborate gateways of Michael Graves, and preoccupations with layered space also influenced the design. The approach to the house is ordered in a general S-curve, and one enters the building through a series of space cells, turning at right angles three times until one reaches the centre with its cross-axis marked on the floor (7). The sequence of framed spaces provides a degree of privacy and surprise, but also a series of framed views of the ubiquitous pines and oaks, given form by the thick borders of the blue posts and beams (8).

Above:

12, 13 Syncopated proportions, typical of Post-Modern dissonance, are set against Renaissance regularities – the three:nine:five rhythm focuses the view on the problem of the corner.

I used the colour red only twice. It indicates, symbolically, the electricity meter at one end of the studio, and draws attention to the sky at the other. When the widow's walk (a traditional Massachusetts balcony on the roof) seemed too squat, we added mouldings to make it flare out. Since prefabricated doors and screens (thirteen in all) were used extensively, it was necessary to pick out the actual entrance, so a conventional pediment marks the 'front door'. And, since these ready-made pediments are rather kitsch versions of eighteenth-century prototypes, it was stripped of its demi-pineapple and doubled to give a 'twice-broken split pediment'. To get rid of central door jambs, which would have blocked a clear view to the main balcony deck, three glass doors were fixed together as a wall and slung as a travelling barn door which, when open, slides into the overall entrance frame. Thus there is a redundancy of doors – doors to heighten the act of entry, exit or transition. It could have been called the DOOR HOUSE, were it not named the GARAGIA ROTUNDA.

The inside space is modulated by surprising variations. Windows are sometimes at floor level to pick up views under the bushes, a baldacchino-like space is formed by the interior steps and the garage door (when it is open), and rhythmical harmonies are formed by the studs that support the walls. The four-by-four inch stud is used here partly decoratively and partly to emphasise the three:nine:five rhythm of the side walls. The sides of each

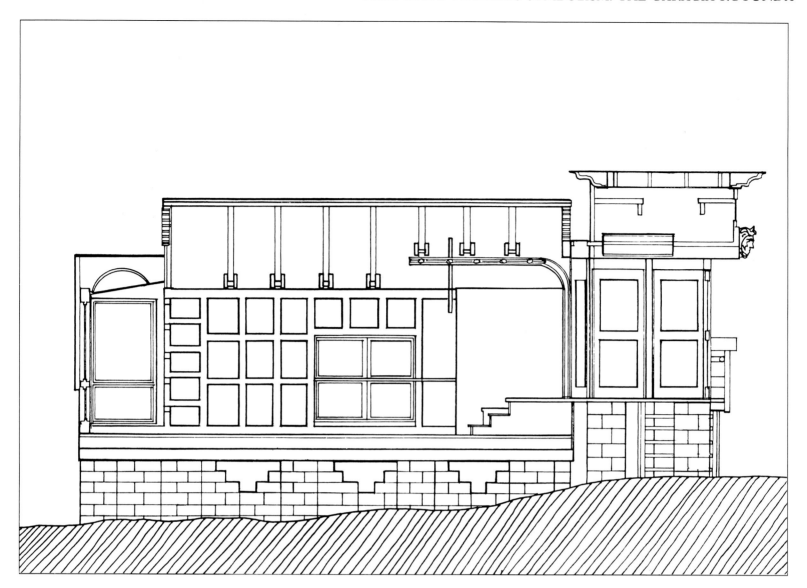

Below:
14, 15   The four-by-four inch stud becomes a chair and its cushion. The quick logic studies show several variations before the final solution (*bottom centre*) was reached.

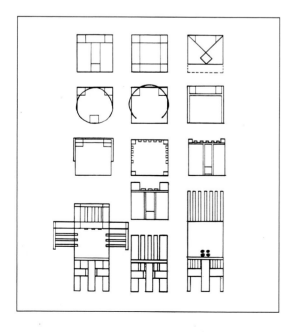

stud are painted in increasingly saturated hues of blue as they approach the internal corner (12,13). This is to dramatise 'the problem of the corner' (for which there is no correct Classical solution). The internal corner is painted to resemble a mirror (with a dropped stud) and this *trompe l'oeil* emphasises the problem with which every Classicist has wrestled.

Several other structural elements establish harmonic relationships, but these are not systematised; rather, they are set in counterpoint or syncopation. Throughout, Classical parts are used freely. If a straight revivalist were composing the wall proportions, he would harmonise the ratios: *concinnatus*, the principle of concord between all parts, would be his goal. Here, by contrast, the parts are internally harmonious, but discordant with respect to one another. Dissonance set against an established consonance is a recurrent idea in Post-Modernism.

The furniture is also made with four-by-four inch studs, again painted in various blues to distinguish major from minor components (14,15). The three-legged chair, like those of Frank Lloyd Wright which it resembles, is rather unstable. If you lean too far forward, or to the left or right, you end up on the floor. But balance can be achieved easily enough by adding your own two legs to those of the chair. Incidentally, the cushion uses the same increasing saturations of blue as the stud wall, so a certain ambiguity is introduced between wood and cushion, hard and soft.

16, 17, 18 Anthropomorphism, explicit and implicit, is apparent in the plan as well as the facades. Wendel Dietterlin, in his redesign of the five columnar orders, also shows this variation.

In several places the image of a face or body is introduced, as in Classical architecture, to create a link with ourselves. Sometimes, as in the plan of the studio, the body image is hidden; at others, as with the Medusa head above the entrance, it is explicit (16). At the rear, the face motif is half-suggested, neither completely explicit nor implicit, but part of several other images (17). Thus it merges with the bay window, the plastic domes set behind a cut-out forehead and the concrete teeth. The pitched-roof face house is a traditional idea which finds expression in both the drawings of children and the detached house. It seems to be a notion that most European countries have followed, and there are examples also in the East. Whatever the history of this subliminal image, its psychological importance is clear: it allows an empathy with inanimate form, the projection of bodily states onto parts of the building – in Classical architecture often the mouldings and columns. Perhaps this projection is an example of the pathetic fallacy. Common speech reveals the metaphor: buildings are said to have a 'front and back', a 'head and foot', and indeed many other parts of the body, including a 'heart'. The advantage of using such metaphors on large-scale housing estates, where people often feel alienated, is obvious. But, it seems to me, the most successful use of anthropomorphic imagery is when there is a subtle alternation between implicit metaphor and explicit simile, between, say, a Classical Ionic column – the *sign* of a young girl – and a caryatid – the *image* of a young girl. This allows the meaning to be felt as well as known.

19, 20 The one-inch rotunda, the ultimate content of the symbolic programme, actually curves enough to be perceptible. As at Palladio's Villa Rotonda, steps mount towards it from the four horizons and main views.

Overleaf:
21 At certain charmed moments, when the sun is right, the shadows all line up geometrically squared and the circle hits the centre-line of the floor and focuses the view.

The GARAGIA ROTUNDA takes its name, finally, from the conjunction of two opposite building types: the lowliest, functional shed, most humble and cheap of covered spaces, and the highest symbolic building task, the heavenly dome or rotunda. Garage and rotunda as a set of contradictory requirements are conventionalised in the house. In Anglo-Saxon countries the rotunda has entered into the history of the villa, palace and then large house through the usage and writings of Andrea Palladio. His Villa Rotonda set the pattern in the sixteenth century by placing a hitherto sacred dome over a secular, centrally planned house. This act of architectural sacrilege, or blasphemy, was soon copied by the English and institutionalised in a way which bore little relationship to the origins of the form – from bath house to pantheon to church to St Peter's and St Paul's to private villa. And thence to the American South and State Capitol buildings.

The GARAGIA ROTUNDA is an ironic comment on the history of this form. It uses the qualities of the rotunda for capturing light and the sky (as a sun-dial which casts a round shadow throughout the day in the studio), and makes a reference to the public nature of the origins of this sign (19,20). Hence its double role. The rotunda is made up from slats of wood, painted in two shades of blue, which step up and inwards to a thin diaphragm of wood which, like the lens of a camera, surrounds the open sky with a dark blue border. The square plan is orientated to the four horizons, as in Palladio's Villa Rotonda. The dome is, however, smaller than Palladio's, in fact it is the smallest dome in Christendom, curving up to catch the sun only seven-eighths of an inch. This curve, and the round shape, are just enough for one to perceive the form as a dome, and quite enough to create a bright circular disk which travels over the geometric floor during the day, marking the hours.

CHAPTER III
The Building as Scenario: The Elemental House

MODERNISM HAS LEFT US HEIRS TO A TRADITION full of beauty and bereft of iconography. Disdainful of convention, Modern architects failed to evolve any system of meaning comparable to the five columnar orders. At best, they produced fine technical and aesthetic solutions, but always of an individual nature. They did not use each others' ordering systems in a conventional and symbolic way to enable the growth of a new tradition comparable to the Classical one they displaced. As a result, their inventions never took root. Those of their columns and orders which were imitated – such as Mies van der Rohe's epochal I-beam, the Doric of Modernism – were supremely non-semantic. Hence Modern architecture, like Modern theatre, has not evolved much beyond the 'grunt and groan' school of expression.

For a long time Post-Modern architects have felt that this aesthetic and technical approach was not enough: a semantic dimension was an obvious and necessary addition to their heritage. In this house in Los Angeles' Rustic Canyon I was fortunate enough to be able to experiment on myself with symbolic ideas. The symbolism uses two themes, interwoven around a house so basic, or fundamental, that I have termed it 'elemental'. One theme develops the idea of the Four Californian Elements – the fact that in California, as in ancient Greece, almost everyone worships the water, land, beautiful views and sun, or in Classical terms, Aqua, Terra, Aer and Ignis (1). At times people seem almost to follow the ancient belief that these are the ultimate elements of the universe. The other theme, inspired by John Milton's two poems 'L'Allegro' and 'Il Penseroso', was suggested by the active and contemplative parts of the existing site. The route through this site is organised around these two themes so that one can follow a symbolic progression, something comparable to a Classical order.

The house, or series of seven pavilions, is situated in a canyon which is aptly named 'rustic' because of its wild eucalyptus trees and rustic buildings, which include many versions of the log cabin, a few examples of what is known locally as the 'woodbutcher's art', and several ranch houses in the laid-back and spread-eagled style. Hence other reasons for the elemental style adopted in my own pavilions.

The first pavilion, the REVERSIBLE GATE, is an entrance gate with two primitive pediments. Instead of the usual split pediment, or double-layered one in the Baroque manner, there are two pediments placed in opposition to one another, in anastrophic relationship. One is upside down, the other

Previous page:
1   View of the AQUA PAVILION through the
TERRA GATE with a Latin inscription from a
programme referring to an earthquake: '*THE
EARTH OPENS UP HER MAW, AND INSTANTLY PERISH
THE HORDES OF KORAH . . .*'

2   REVERSIBLE GATE. The pediments are upside
down and right-side up – visually rotated about
an axis which is picked out by decorated nuts and
bolts. The four quadrants of these forms have
four signs which are clarified in later pavilions.

right-side up, and they hold four enigmatic signs in their four quadrants (2).
These are the first clues to the architectural promenade and the beginning of
the game of 'Hunt the Symbol'. Another expectation is set up by the
elemental Nut-and-Bolt order of piers, the constructional elements of which
are accentuated by shades of pink and red. These slight variations of familiar
shapes are meant to provoke questioning. What is the meaning of the
triangular gable stood on its head? Why are the bolts and washers
accentuated with paint, and what *are* the four emblematic signs?

The second pavilion, the GARAGE-TEMPLE, also a primitive hut, answers
some of these questions while raising new ones (3). It is a garage with a more
developed Nut-and-Bolt order – now openly celebrating Mid-Tech with its
redundant washers, sheet metal and coiling columns of fat culvert pipe (4). It
is the epitome of the garage aesthetic rendered clean and ordered. There are
orders of garbage cans and firewood, of chapels and painted car tracks, all
united by a common geometry (5). And the lettering in the elemental, or
rustic, script is part of the same aesthetic. In the tie-beams of the trusses a new
set of associations is started: '*HENCE LOATHED MELANCHOLY,/ OF CERBERUS AND
BLACKEST MIDNIGHT BORN/ IN STYGIAN CAVE FORLORN,/ 'MONGST HORRID SHAPES,
AND SHRIEKS, AND SIGHTS UNHOLY!/ FIND OUT SOME UNCOUTH CELL,/ WHERE BROOD-
ING DARKNESS SPREADS HIS JEALOUS WINGS,/ AND THE NIGHT RAVEN SINGS.*' These
opening lines from John Milton's 'L'Allegro' are clearly echoed by the dark
and black forms. The 'uncouth cell' holds the firewood and garbage and the
parked cars give appropriate 'shrieks, and sights unholy'. But apart from
these parallels – between poem and architecture, and one elemental pavilion
and the next – it is not yet clear what the plot really is. Some plants are also
picked out, or framed by architectural elements labelled with further lines
from Milton. Gradually the allegorical nature of the site becomes more
apparent – its relation to the active and contemplative sides of creative
'melancholy', as described in 'L'Allegro' and 'Il Penseroso'. These correspond to the noisy and quiet parts of the landscape, or the opposition between
brick paving and green lawn. The interaction of Milton's poems with the
Four Elements produces a double semantics: two interwoven sets of meaning.

3   GARAGE-TEMPLE. This distyle temple for cars
has six chapels on the sides which alternate with
piers. The entablature level is left empty – no
metopes – thus making the structure more open
to light and space. Car tracks are painted to aid
parking and are combined with the entablature
and pier order. The opening of Milton's 'L'Allegro', transcribed in rustic lettering, describes a
dark, cave-like cell.

4   GARAGE-TEMPLE, Nut-and-Bolt order. The
black steel constructional element, which unites
pier and architrave, is imitated in wood which is
also painted black. False bolts and washers,
painted in shades of grey and green, complete
the form and give it visual logic. The Doric
temple imitated constructional reality, using
stone to represent wood for visual and logical,
not constructional, reasons.

5   GARAGE-TEMPLE. The chapels are in counterpoint to the piers, and the painted car tracks
repeat the architrave order. The colours – black
and green below, and blue above – relate to
Milton's poem as well as to the surrounding
context.

HENCE LOATHED MELANCHOLY, OF CERBERUS AND BLACKEST MIDNIGHT BORN.

IN STYGIAN CAVE FORLORN, MONGST HORRID SHAPES AND SHRIEKS, AND SIGHTS UNHOLY,

FIND OUT SOME UNCOUTH CELL, WHERE BROODING DARKNESS

SPREADS HIS JEALOUS WINGS, AND THE NIGHT-RAVEN SINGS.

8, 9 The Californian Pool asserts its jagged shape in the brick, emphasising the themes of earth and water. Pool lights indicate major cities such as Los Angeles and Eureka.

6, 7 TERRA GATE. Six quick logic studies were made to determine the most felicitous interaction of function (swing doors), meaning (earthquake represented by a cracked pyramid) and image (a focus through a stylised palm tree). The built solution (*bottom right on drawing*) shows the rustic lettering spelling out the repeated terror of the earthquake.

This becomes clearer in the third pavilion, the TERRA GATE, which has the name of its Californian element repeated in rustic lettering on the architrave, as if to say 'terror, terror, terror . . .' (6,7). Two ancient signs of Terra, the ziggurat and pyramid, have fractures running through them so that this Californian element becomes not earth, but earthquake, an indication that a tributary of the San Andreas fault lies nearby. As one walks through this gate, the earth-coloured brick splits apart to reveal water – Aqua – a swimming pool which is, conveniently, in the shape of California (8,9). The pool also has a jagged line of rupture, a reminder of the fractures in the gate. The Four Elements are not only admired and worshipped here, as they were in Greece, but also feared: water often brings annual mud-slides, fire is a constant threat in the dry foothills . . . and everyone has heard where air pollution was invented.

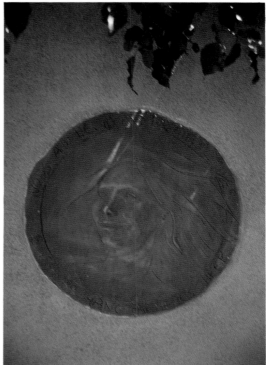

10, 11 'Hebe', personified by Penny Jencks, looks to the left at the flowers winding up the LA columns – a growing order of *Bignonia violaceae*, the 'nods and becks' of Milton's poem.

Once through the gate, the promenade turns right and returns to Milton. Ahead is another eyecatcher, a sculpted relief, with the incised lines: 'NODS AND BECKS AND WREATHED SMILES / SUCH AS HANG ON HEBE'S CHEEK' (10,11). 'Hebe' does smile and look to her left, to the 'nods and becks' (*Bignonia violaceae*) which grow up the LA columns and to the next eyecatcher at the end of the pergola behind the fourth primitive hut – the AQUA PAVILION. Here there can be no ambiguity of meaning. The pavilion is labelled AQUAQUAQUAQUA like a quacking duck and it shelters an automated spa, or jacuzzi (12,13). Water foams and bubbles below a personification of Aqua, a stylised version of Cesare Ripa's *Iconologia*. Certain liberties are taken with the icon: for example she holds a steamboat over her shoulder instead of the customary sailing rig. The pleasure of swimming in Californian Aqua is one of the reasons people continue to settle here. Surfers are perhaps more dedicated to the worship of water than were the ancients.

12 AQUA PAVILION. The jacuzzi has a simple Tuscan order of telephone poles and sheet metal surmounted by an architrave and layered pediment in blue and grey.

13 AQUA PAVILION. Over the jacuzzi is a personification of Aqua by Charles Moore. She rides above the waves and holds a steamboat over one shoulder.

14 AER PAVILION. The basic Tuscan order, made from telephone poles and sheet metal, holds a pediment with the sculpture of Aer flying. The pavilion can open out onto the garden on two sides and the pool in front.

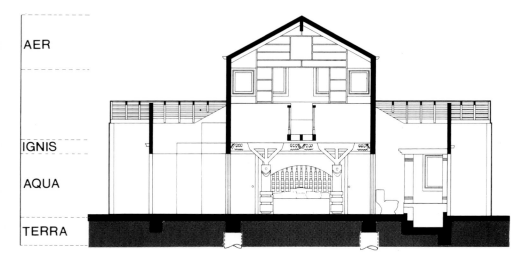

AER

IGNIS

AQUA

TERRA

16 AER PAVILION. The section east–west shows the double-height space focused on the bed, below, and the bookshelves above. The organisational principle of a face can be discerned.

15　The LA columns in the AER PAVILION bedroom are dressed with curtains which block out the light and act as an enclosure for the bed. The red capitals have stylised signs of fire and sunlight. In the background can be seen the stencil of the Four Elements.

The AER PAVILION, the fifth, is in the same style as the others, but is more brightly painted and more elaborately ornamented as it is the culmination of this particular route (14). As one of the main bedrooms, it necessarily has a more delicate order than elsewhere; the LA column dressed outside with a growing pink flower – *Bignonia violaceae* – is dressed inside with pink curtains (15). The order is also more refined, so that like the progression from Doric to Ionic to Corinthian in a Classical temple, there is an ordered sequence, beginning with the REVERSIBLE GATE, from the most primitive to the most developed. Ultimately the orders in architecture do imply an order, and in the AER PAVILION even the ornament follows this progression: the Four Elements are organised vertically. At the bottom are the terra cotta floor tiles. Above these, the water level of the lower walls is symbolised by shades of blue (16). Then comes the fire level of the columns and stencil, and finally, on the ceiling where it should be, is Aer, stencilled and stylised in blue-grey, linear battens (17).

17a, 17b AER PAVILION. Aer is stylised on the ridge-beam with the U-shaped sign first found at the REVERSIBLE GATE. The beams and battens form a rhythmical system of blue-grey shapes that march down the ridge-beam towards the personification of Aer outside.

The themes of the ELEMENTAL HOUSE are clearly explained by the ornament, painting and sculpture in the pavilion. The Four Elements, or rather personifications of them painted by Sidney Hurwitz, occupy the four corners of the lower walls (18,19). What was implicit at the beginning of the journey is now explicit: the notion of fourness within the REVERSIBLE GATE and the enigmatic emblems on each of its quadrants are labelled on the central window above the bath. The Shower Curtain Key, an architectural key like that on a map, is provided as a reward for taking up the initial challenge of 'Hunt the Symbol'. And the stylised arches found in various guises throughout the journey also become meaningful in the bathroom. This form, the Jencksiana arch and stagger, first appeared in the TERRA GATE and then on sconces and furniture. It finally becomes the Bathroom Face, a 'face' in the place that faces are looked at every morning, the bathroom mirror (20). Vanity of vanities, the vanity-mirror has a profile adopted from Michelangelo and Scamozzi, although here it is rude, crude and barbarous rather than elegant; it is impossible to cut a mirror like the profile of a stone cornice. But it does

Above:
18, 19 *Ignis* and *Aqua* on either side of the Shower Curtain Key.

Below:
20, 21   The curve and stagger is used throughout the buildings, ornament and lettering.

make the explicit connection of architecture and the body, an analogy Michelangelo recommended, and thus serves to highlight other anthropomorphic meanings wherever the arch and stagger motif is found on the site. There are three different tables using this form, as well as lamps, wardrobe drawers, various chairs and the collar for a plant. The motif is used so often in different ways that it becomes another variation on a theme, a semantic system in itself (21).

One intention I had when designing these buildings – a polemical point because it sprang more from the then current position of architecture than the programme of the house itself – was to use ornament and sculpture semantically, not just aesthetically. So much decoration in this stormy age of ornamentalism is just poured over buildings as if this downpour would compensate for the previous drought. But meaningless ornament is as pointless as none at all – it just confuses the architecture. Hence when working on the pavilions and gardens, along with Buzz Yudell and Maggie Keswick, I tried to insist on a thematic programme before the sculpture was made.

Die Lufft.

Opposite:
22, 23 *Aer*, sheet metal sculpture by Timothy Woodman. Cesare Ripa describes her as parting the clouds as she flies, catching the sun's rays in her hair 'signifying the beneficial aspects of the air, which transmits the sun's rays to man'. These meanings and the surrounding context have inspired the polychromy.

Above:
24 Cesare Ripa, *Aer*. 'Elijah is carried aloft across the reaches of the sky; no one excelled him in piety'.

25 AER PAVILION, frieze of the Californian elements. Earth runs along the bottom, water and fire bubble above, while the sign of Aer provides a rhythmical punctuation. The analogy is of ornament as a repeated musical theme.

Overleaf:
26, 27 IGNIS PAVILION. The faces table has a sectioned log with annual rings which represent the sun. Behind this are two face chairs, sunburst lights and Roland Coate's painting *Baja Sands*. The face chairs exploit hand-crafted production but the result is modified to make them more stable and fitting for their context.

In certain cases, such as the personification of Aer by Timothy Woodman, the thematic design was, I believe, very successful (22,23). Woodman has taken Cesare Ripa's model and description of Aer – 'a pretty young girl dressed in draperies of transparent white, with wings on her shoulders . . .' – and transformed it in material and colour. Because of the sheet metal, because of the surrounding greens, oranges and reds, and because it is the twentieth and not the sixteenth century, Aer is not an exact transcription of the type (24). In every case the artists working on the house were asked to reinterpret traditional programmes to bring them to life; not to copy them but to transform them. Working to a symbolic programme is, of course, unusual for a twentieth-century artist nurtured on the autonomy of art and the idea that the proper subject-matter of painting is the recent history of art and its formal essence – for example 'flatness' or 'painterliness'. Nevertheless, I have found that here, as elsewhere, there is a latent desire among artists to return to an iconographic programme – if it is relevant, and if they can shape it. Admittedly, the Four Elements may seem arcane at first, especially since we now know of one hundred and four, but it does have a relevance to southern California where people still flock in because of the sun, land, space and sea. The fact that here each of these mythical elements has its drawbacks only adds to their symbolic power.

One more polemical point might be made about the AER PAVILION and its ornament. The decorative frieze, combining the Four Elements, is a repeat pattern designed as a musical figure with a treble and base, or a high and low register, and emphatic phrasing (25). The figures line up and their visual force, exploding from the centre, runs to each side and the punctuation point, the Sign of Aer. The scheme is intended to give what Owen Jones and E.H. Gombrich identify as the aesthetic essence of ornament – a pull towards the expected goal, a drive towards the main key or tonic. So the ornament is not simply semantic, or a literal transcription of the signs at the front gate, but a stylisation of them to give aesthetic momentum.

The AER PAVILION is the culmination of one plot, the Four Californian Elements. The other plot, the poems, continues further around the landscape and through the pavilions. It would be laborious to give a line-by-line, flower-by-flower description of this walk, and in any case the poems have not been completely followed. There is still much missing and, inevitably, a lot more present, but the interested reader can consult the plan at the end of this chapter. Only in a church will one find anything approaching complete correspondence between architecture and storyline, art and liturgy. Nonetheless, there is enough correspondence here to keep the plot developing. 'L'Allegro' continues into the living room of the IGNIS PAVILION, a 1952 ranch house stripped to its essentials and repainted in light colours. Here the themes of the poem and of California are combined in a light, white room filled with allusions to previous themes: for instance within one table are primitive signs of the sun and several transformations of the face (26). The paintings of Roland Coate, particularly his *Baja Sands*, bring out the white bleaching light of California. Sunburst lamps provide a literal reminder of the Ignis-sun connection, and because this is the IGNIS PAVILION (with its fire-red chimney) there are many other signs of the sun. Heavy logs, cut in short lengths to reveal their annual rings, are painted a sandy cream to represent the sun, while two sunburst chairs, remodelled and accentuated in their curves, are both 'faces' and haloes of the sun (27).

From the main house, the journey continues through the second poem, 'Il Penseroso', a celebration of the creative melancholy of the poet. Here the soft garden side of the site comes to the forefront. Where before everything was hard and fixed, now it is pliable and growing: a giant, statuesque palm dominates one vista, along with leaning acacia and eucalyptus trees (28). The late afternoon sun sends long shadows across the flat green of the lawn. On a direct axis from the house is the tibouchina plant with its purple petals and velvety leaves. This represents the positive side of melancholy – in the poem a 'goddess, sage and holy,' – while her imaginary parents, Vesta and Saturn, are represented by a white magnolia and the thorned trunk of *Chorissa speciosa*. From here the garden path meanders back and forth, taking up further lines of 'Il Penseroso' until it culminates in the seventh and last pavilion, the HERMITAGE.

It is worth quoting several lines of Milton to bring out aspects of the architecture. Milton's hermitage is described essentially as a peaceful scholar's retreat, part church with a cloister and part 'mossy cell' for the hermit poet:

> *'But let my due feet never fail,/To walk the studious cloister's pale,*
> *And love the high embowed roof,/With antique pillars massyproof.'*

The HERMITAGE, as built, does have a cloister and high roof, and although the pillars are not antique, or exactly Classical, they are massive (29). (Actually they take up the primitive Tuscan order, in sheet metal, of the other pavilions.)

Above:
28 The garden, with the 1952 ranch house (IGNIS PAVILION) to the left, the palm in the background and tibouchina, magnolia and *Chorissa speciosa* to the right.

29 HERMITAGE. The bedroom is church-like with tabernacle windows, a central cross over the doorway, a 'cloister' with LA columns and a large Tuscan porch.

30 HERMITAGE, plan and elevation. A Latin cross-plan focuses on the bed, door and exterior seat. The 'cloister' is defined by the piers and tiled squares. Ferns grow in the tiers of the mini-amphitheatre.

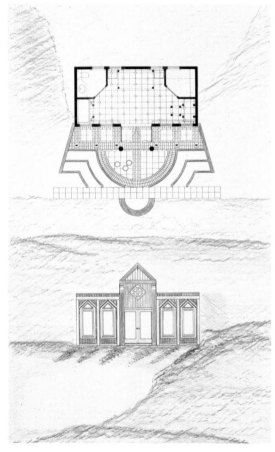

Inside, Milton described the hermitage as having clerestory windows that cast 'a dim religious light'. Here the light from above is hardly dim, but the space is given many religious accents including a window-cross over the door and a baldacchino-like shape over the bed (31). Indeed the bed, bath alcove, chair and table are all miniature churches, with elemental religious signs and a cathedral plan (30). Even the tabernacle windows, and interwoven ornament which derive from them, have religious overtones.

'There let the pealing organ blow,/To the full-voiced quire below,
In service high, and anthems clear,/As may with sweetness, through mine ear,
Dissolve me into ecstasies,/And bring all heaven before mine eyes.'

Those who have slept in this bedroom, tucked away in the garden and insulated from the noise and bustle of the main house, do value its contemplative calm. This is created partly by white-pink colouring and the very simple geometric order – a Latin cross in plan. And partly it is a result of the light spilling through the trees and the canopy of glass above the bed (32). The HERMITAGE, like all the other pavilions, is basically a very simple primitive hut with a fundamental LA order incised into the furniture (33,34). It completes the journey as the last element in the ELEMENTAL HOUSE and brings us back to the GARAGE-TEMPLE at the beginning of the route.

If there is one obvious problem with the building as scenario it concerns the danger of overdesign: it is difficult to know where to stop representing further and further ideas. This can lead to certain anomalies such as the private bedroom which may become too formal and public, or the modest

31, 32 HERMITAGE. The bed is designed as a miniature shrine. It sits below a canopy of glass that focuses on the cross over the door. All the pavilions open out to nature – a Californian tradition – and frame it architecturally.

33, 34 HERMITAGE. The chair and table stand below David Remfrey's painting *Melancholy* which features the tibouchina plant in the garden.

35-38 A symbolic garden in its early develop-ment. The passive and active (*opposite top and above*) parts of the garden are characterised by the two poems 'Il Penseroso' and 'L'Allegro'. Around the TERRA GATE are three citrus trees symbolising the three Graces: Euphrosyne (tangerine), Aglaia (orange) and Thalia (lemon). Euphrosyne, or Mirth, can be seen (*far left*) framed by dark red volumes and stencilled words from the poem: '*BUT COME THOU GODDESS FAIR AND FREE,/IN HEAVEN YCLEPT EUPHROSYNE,/AND BY MEN HEART-EASING MIRTH*'. Other garden furni-ture also has phrases referring to the plants and their connection with the poem. For instance the lines '*SPORT THAT WRINKLED CARE DERIDES,/AND LAUGHTER HOLDING BOTH HIS SIDES*' are symbol-ised in the overgrown fuschia and truncated obelisk (*left*). Lettering, architecture and planting all illustrate different aspects of the same meaning.

backroom which may accidentally turn into a grandiose state room. Probably not more than one-third of a house should have a full symbolic programme. The advantages of following a plot are really found in the drama engendered. Architecture, like theatre, is best experienced as a steady build-up of narrative, where the story impels one forward to anticipate and then seek out further incidents which relate to the main theme. A large Egyptian temple complex provides the drama of anticipation and fulfilment, just as a Gothic cathedral provides a clear temporal and visual build-up near the high altar. The tradition of designing a dramatic walk though a site has been extended by Mannerist gardeners, who no doubt gave unity to their plots with an overall idea, a *concetto*, or concept. One can still find very effective use of this 'idea of the idea' at the Villa Lante and Bomarzo, both gardens whose plots have been partially decoded. The Picturesque English garden was also composed as a set of discrete frames, or pictures, to which one could add captions as one strolled through it. The idea of labelling such a sequence so that architecture and the theatre exert their full powers of temporal drama has yet to be fully attempted. Something close to it has been realised in the classic Chinese garden, but no one has fully exploited the combination.

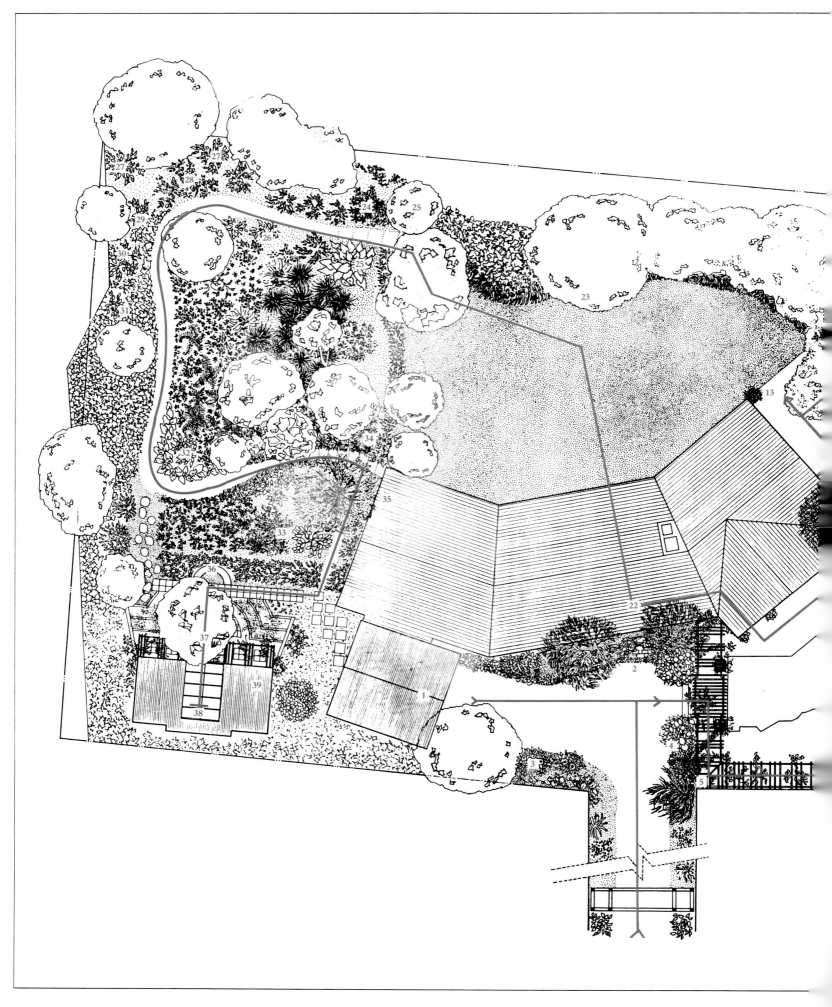

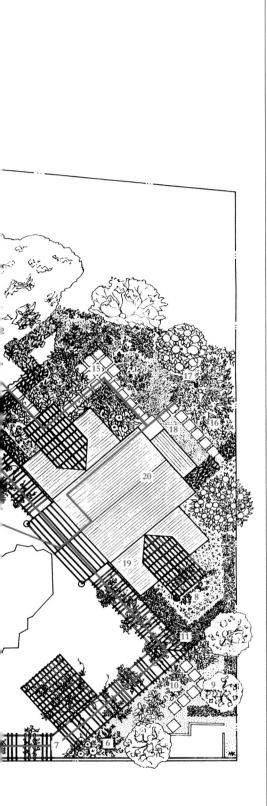

L'Allegro

1

'Hence loathèd melancholy
Of Cerberus, and *blackest midnight* born,
In Stygian cave forlorn
'Mongst *horrid shapes,* and shrieks,
and *sights unholy,*'
(Blackest midnight: black and dark
green colouring. Horrid shapes and
sights unholy: noisy polluting automobiles parked here and garbage stored
in sewer pipes painted black and green.)

2

'. . . Come thou goddess fair and free,
In heaven yclept *Euphrosyne,*
And by men, heart-easing mirth,'
(The three Greek Graces are personified
as three Californian citrus trees:
tangerine for Euphrosyne (mirth),
lemon for Aglaia (brilliance) and orange
for Thalia (bloom). All three trees are
ever-blooming and ever-fruiting.)

3

'Whom lovely *Venus* at a birth
With two sister Graces more
To ivy-crownèd *Bacchus* bore;'
(Venus: pink and white semi-formal
camellia with perfect petals, but tightly
closed heart. Bacchus: grape ivy grown
all over the fence behind Venus.)

4

'Or whether (as some sager sing)
The frolic wind that breathes the spring,
Zephyr, with *Aurora* playing,
As he met her once a-Maying,
There on beds of *violets blue,*
And fresh-blown *roses* washed in dew.'
(Zephyr: *Agonis flexuosa,* the willow
myrtle, because its fine leaves move in
the slightest breeze. Aurora: an
American *Bougainvillea,* 'Texas Dawn'.
The violets blue are massed in beds
under the climbing rose 'Cecile
Brunner'.)

5

'Haste thee nymph, and bring with thee
Jest and *youthful jollity,*
Quips and cranks, and wanton wiles,
Nods, and becks, and wreathèd smiles,
Such as hang on *Hebe's* cheek . . .'
(Youthful jollity, nods and becks: little
orange cumquats and nodding violet
Bignonia violaceae planted all along the
pergola. Hebe: a relief of the goddess of
youth's head is set into the wall beneath
the vines and bignonia.)

6

'And laughter *holding both his sides* . . .'
(A fat-bellied pot set on a stand with a
decorated base suggesting hands.)

7

'And in thy right hand lead with thee,
The *mountain nymph,* sweet liberty,'
(Mountain nymph: native white tree
anemone *Carpenteria California,* which
grows wild over the hills in California.)

8

'. . . At my window bid good morrow,
Through the *sweetbriar or the vine,*
Or the twisted *eglantine.*'
(*Rosa eglanteria* and wisteria vines twist
up the pillars of the Eastern porch.)

9

'While the *cock* with lively din,
Scatters the rear of darkness thin . . .'
(Antique windvane of a cockerel.)

10

'While . . . the *milkmaid* singeth blithe,
And the *mower* whets his scythe . . .'
(Milkmaid: huge milky cups of
Magnolia soiulangeana. Mower: hay-
scented fern, *Dennstaedtia punctilibula.*)

11

'And every *shepherd* tells his tale
Under the *hawthorn* in the dale.'
(The pink geranium 'Shepherd's
Morning' planted under a hedge of the
Indian hawthorn, *Raphiolepsis Indica*
'Spring-time'.)

12

'Where the *nibbling flocks* do stray . . .'
(*Stachys lanata,* or 'lambs' ears'.)

13

'*Meadows trim* with *daisies* pied,
Shallow brooks, and rivers wide.
Towers, and battlements it sees
Bosomed high in tufted trees . . .'
(View encompassing big pots of tree
daisies, the lawn, canyon, stream and
houses among old trees.)

14

'Hard by, a *cottage chimney* smokes,
From betwixt *two aged oaks,*
Where Corydon and Thyrsis met,
Are at their *savory dinner* set'
(The cottage chimney of our next door
neighbour's rustic house is just visible
behind evergreen Californian live oaks.
This is where we eat dinner outside.)

15

'Of *herbs* and other country messes . . .'
(Herbs: rosemary, thyme and rugosa
roses.)

16

'When the *merry bells* ring round . . .'
(Merry bells: pink abutilon bells.)

17

'Dancing in the *chequered shade* . . .
Till the livelong daylight fail,
Then to the *spicy nut-brown ale* . . .'
(Chequered shade and spicy ale: pepper
tree *Schinus terebinthi folius.*)

18

'And he by *friar's lantern* led . . .'
(The friar's, or fairy lantern, is
Calochortus albus.)

19

'Tells how the drudging *goblin* sweat
To earn his cream-bowl duly set . . .'
(Goblin's face in mirrors of bathroom.)

20

'Thus done the tales, to bed they creep,
By whispering winds soon lulled asleep.'
(Bedroom.)

21

'Towered cities please us then . . .
With store of *ladies, whose bright eyes*
Rain influence . . .
There let *Hymen* oft appear . . .'
(Ladies: hibiscus 'Lady Baltimore' and
camellia 'Mrs W. D. Davis'. Bright
eyes: star jasmine. Hymen: *Stephanotis,*
flower of wedding bouquets.)

22

'Then to the well-trod stage anon . . .'
(Table with comic and tragic masks.)

Il Penseroso

23

'. . . Hail thou goddess, sage and holy,
Hail, divinest *melancholy,*'
(Melancholy: *Tibouchina urvilleana,*
which has velvety leaves and royal
purple flowers.)

24

'. . . Starred *Ethiope* queen . . .'
(*Magnolia stellata.*)

25

'Thee bright-hair'd *Vesta* long of yore,
To solitary *Saturn* bore . . .'
(Vesta is symbolised by calla lillies,
Saturn by *Chorissa speciosa* with its
massive thorned trunk and the rose
'Maiden's Blush' is behind them.)

26

'Come *pensive nun,* devout and pure,
Sober, steadfast, and demure . . .'
(Camellia 'White Nun' underplanted
with white azalea 'Màdonna'.)

27

'And join with thee calm *peace,* and *quiet,*'
(Camellias with closed centre petals.)
'*Spare fast,* that oft with gods doth diet,'
(Very small-flowered, leggy camellia.)

28

'And hears the *Muses* in a ring,
Aye round about Jove's altar sing.'
(Muses: three roses facing a semi-
circular table under a tall tree.)

29, 30, 31

'And add to these retired *leisure,*
That in trim gardens takes his pleasure;
But, first and chiefest, with thee bring,
. . . The *cherub* contemplation,
And the mute *silence* hist along . . .'
(All are camellias: leisure is large and
floppy, the cherub small and chubby,
silence closed.)

32

'While *Cynthia* checks her dragon yoke,
Gently o'er the accustomed oak . . .'
(Cynthia, goddess of the moon, is
suggested by a camellia called
'Moonlight Bay'.)

33

'Oft on a plat of rising ground,
I hear the far-off curfew sound,
Over some *wide-watered shore* . . .'
(From the higher ground here the
distant Pacific Ocean is clearly audible,
and the slope is planted with a cream-
coloured polyantha rose called 'Sea
Foam'.)

34

'Where *glowing embers* through the room
Teach light to counterfeit a gloom,'
(All the shady groves under the trees
planted with *Clivia.*)

35

'. . . Let my lamp at midnight hour
Be seen in some *high lonely tower* . . .'
(The end of the main house, though not
a tower, is on the highest part of the
slope here.)
'. . . Those demons that are found
In *fire, air, flood,* or under *ground* . . .'
(Refers back to the four elemental
pavilions.)

36

All the tales of tragedy and songs of
Orpheus in the poem are suggested by
the little amphitheatre in front of the
guest house.

37

'Thus, *night,* see oft me in thy pale career
Till civil suited *morn* appear . . .'
(Night: moon vines. Morn: morning
glories planted over pergola with
jasmine and wisteria.)

38

'But let my due feet never fail,
To walk the studious *cloister's* pale,
And love the high *embowe'd roof,*
With antique pillars *massy-proof,*
And *storied windows* richly dight . . .
Find out the peaceful hermitage,
The hairy gown and mossy cell . . .'
(The guest house was designed to fit this
description.)

39

'These pleasures *melancholy* give,
And I with thee will choose to live.'
(A portrait of melancholy hangs inside
the guest house above the desk, and her
symbol, *Tibouchina urvilleana,* is planted
again outside.)

CHAPTER IV
Interlude
PART I: THE FACE OF THE VERNACULAR

1, 2 The ruined walls are capped in red stone and the blue-grey slate of the roof is echoed by the trellis. Addition and subtraction, burnt-out ruin and renovation, are the rhetorical contrasts equivalent to the local vernacular black on white.

3 Symmetry focuses the view on the major axis.

T HESE TWO SMALL CONVERSIONS WERE DESIGNED only partially to symbolic programmes, but they reflect the same thinking and style as the other schemes. They are built parts of larger buildings, interventions on a minor scale, rather than totalities of architecture, craftsmanship and art. The Face of the Vernacular is the partial conversion of a farm building in Dumfriesshire. The buildings in this part of Scotland are often red or rubble stone, or masonry painted white. When white, they are usually trimmed with black corners which serve both as a visual stop and as an accentuation of the cut-stone quoins. The results are most curious – the corners resemble a heavy saw-tooth, or rustication, or even steps to climb. This black and white vernacular is in vivid contrast to

the soft rolling green of the hills. It may seem a bit far-fetched, but one could imagine the countless small buildings dotting the vast open landscape as tiny Greek temples lost in giant, treeless sites – again, a rhetoric of extreme contrast.

In this renovation and conversion, the strongly contrasting language of the Scottish farm building is used on a smaller scale and in wood so that it continues to relate to the existing vernacular while letting in more light. The vernacular is given a new face – or the abstract representation of a face – by means of the exact symmetry about the stair. This, in forced perspective, draws the eye up to the triangular window and thence to the open triangular gable, which will later hold a climbing rose – a Scottish rose. Thus the physical ascension is accompanied by an architectural one, ending in the blue sky framed by a black trellis. The colour of the trellis harmonises with the slate roof, and while it is as gloomy as the black windows of the local vernacular, it is given relief by the contrast of the white and the stone, and by the future rose. Thus the natural oppositions within the local style are played on and heightened.

One example of this is the addition to the barn roof and the subtraction of part of the crumbled wall. Another is the protrusion of part of the white

4 The stair/seat repeats in miniature the face pattern of the house.

5 The forced perspective pulls the eye upwards to the two triangular shapes which continue the movement.

6 The stair: a nervous staccato of two to one and four to one.

7 On the top floor, the door enframes the major view, while the windows let in more north light: the space may be used as a studio in the future.

stair across the gate to the courtyard. A third example is the opposition between the thin black, busy lines of the stairs and window frames and the overall peaceful outline. This agitation is increased by the subtle shifts in rhythm – two to one in the vertical railings, and four to one in the pergola. So variety is set against regularity; for instance the box seats which visually and physically hold the stair also repeat the overall face pattern in miniature.

The basic constructional element, the four-by-four inch stud, is used partly in a redundant way in the interior to set up primary ratios: one to one, three to one, four to one. These geometrical forms are then accentuated by painting the sides of the studs darker shades of blue nearer the edge. In these ways the very basic elements of the vernacular – the construction, the wall and the view – are clearly defined. The method was used previously in the Garagia Rotunda.

Since the final use of the building has not yet been determined, the symbolism is at present confined to the language itself – the vernacular. On further development, a symbolic programme might determine the ornament, and the building will be completed by dotting the 'i's and doubling the doorknobs.

PART II: THE STUDIOLO

THIS RENOVATION OF A VERY SMALL ROOM AT THE top of a London house is for a boy who has an interest in sports and may someday go into public life as a businessman or statesman. The room – a seven-foot cube with a west-facing window – had to function as a bedroom and study. The symbolic programme for the design of the room stresses both the active and contemplative life: an interest in BMW bikes, wild birds and shooting on the one hand, and reading, sleeping and thinking on the other.

To increase the sense of space and break up the cube, a round window was cut into the middle of the wall and a cruciform of mirrors placed on the ceiling on axis with the windows. A long mirror opposite the original west-facing window allows views to the outside from any point in the room, and all the reflective surfaces pick up the main cross-axes, reinforce the square geometry, centralise the wall motifs and symbolise the contemplative realm (reflective gazing as one lies in bed) – which they are also supposed to aid.

Six flights of stairs lead to this eyrie, the last arriving at a door ornamented with patterns based on stylised telescopes and a schematic bird – a swift – that also resembles a face. The same bird appears again inside the room, this time even more like a face. Like his father, the owner is an expert at identifying birds. Turning round he can see in the design on the back of the door his initials – C H – and a D for Door.

8   Entrance. The door to the right has a stylised swift above telescopes to set the theme of bird-watching. The wardrobe has a swift/face image.

9   Desk/bed with postcard frieze. The postcards show famous statesmen and sportsmen.

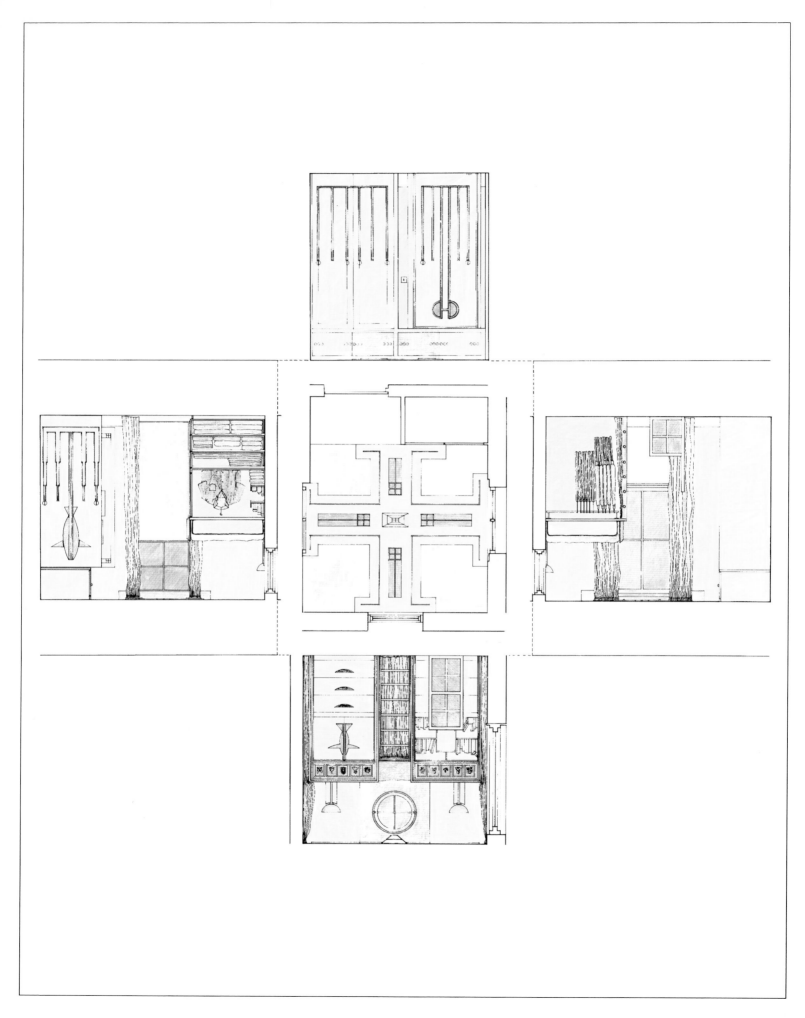

Opposite:
10 Four facades and reflective ceiling plan.

Above:
11 Wardrobe doorknobs resemble the tops of growing plants. Practical elements such as knobs are doubled and tripled to become rhythmical motifs.

12 The door closes to reveal the occupant's initials – C H – and D for Door.

13, 14 The overhead light and ceiling mirrors take up the main cross-axes.

The desk/wardrobe/bed takes up the whole of one side of the room, with the door and cupboards on the opposite wall. A frieze of postcards marches along the side of the bed, celebrating figures from the worlds of sport, history and politics: as the owner's taste changes, he can change the cards. Doors open below the frieze, drawers and a desk top slide out, and a secret storage area is hidden behind the ladder. Like a traditional *studiolo*, the room is a magical box of tricks. The real window overlooking London rooftops is reflected in the 'window mirror' opposite, both of them hung with curtains. Thus the room's size is expanded, and what was a low, cramped, dark and rather dismal space has become a bright and interesting room with a number of uses.

CHAPTER V
Towards a Symbolic Architecture: The Thematic House

1 THEMATIC HOUSE from the street, night view. The two chimneys, London columns, focus the west elevation over an S-curved roof, a Hildebrandtian motif, while the arched windows, face motifs, focus the views out of the house onto the trees.

2 Front door with its stylised body, head and initials of all the family. The letter-box is the heart.

THE THEMATIC HOUSE IN LONDON IS OUR MOST sustained attempt to face directly the question of meaning. What, in this agnostic age, is there to symbolise beyond the perennial themes of comfort and fashion? It would be difficult for me to sustain a belief in any point of religious dogma – to design a house based, like Tresham's Triangular Lodge, on the Trinity, for example – while the themes selected by twentieth-century architects, such as Frank Lloyd Wright in his Hollyhock House, seem limited in range. Historically, we are placed at a point of scepticism – scientists, cosmologists and theologians cannot even begin to agree on the nature of the universe – and many recent architects have celebrated relatively trivial subjects. We have therefore chosen an historical perspective that represents time, both cosmic and everyday. Instead of proclaiming certainties of belief, we use the hypotheses of science and conventional wisdom as guides. The notion is that even in a secular age, there are still objective standards worthy of symbolic expression in architecture, art and ornament, and these are the standards by which we orientate ourselves.

The THEMATIC HOUSE is the reworking of an 1840s building that ends a short row of three 'late-Georgian' terrace houses. Because of the context, the existing grammar of the surrounding buildings had to be respected and we made only small variations on their themes for the house's facade. But as one circles the house, from public street front to semi-public side to more private garden, this grammar becomes more and more expressive and individual (1): for instance the top floor dormer windows on the front, which resemble those of our neighbour, are at the back multiplied to express one of the important themes of the house – the suggestion of a face.

The front door of the THEMATIC HOUSE also has a stylised face where other Georgian houses might have a fanlight. Below it, mouldings suggest abstractions of the body (the hands signalled by two doorknobs) surrounded by abstractions of all the family's initials – C, J, M, L – some of them back to front (2). I have tried to keep most of the symbols abstract or relatively hidden since, unlike painting or literature, architecture cannot afford to tell a story the whole time. It must be background as well as foreground, and so far as symbolism is concerned, I have adopted a strategy of abstract representation, stylising the salient parts of an image (for example the eyes, nose and mouth of a face) then generalising them into geometric forms which can be varied endlessly. There is a face house in Japan which is so literal that the front door swallows the inhabitant every night. More satisfactory to me are the subliminal face houses found in Amsterdam or Northern European countries, which allow one to feel the imagery before noticing it. The face and body have been architectural themes since the Egyptians first based their buildings on the image and measurements of the human figure, and the obvious virtue of this anthropomorphism is that of humanising inert matter. We quite naturally empathise with buildings which allow us to project our bodily state onto them.

Once through this 'human door', one arrives at the COSMIC OVAL, a space panelled with mirrored doors above which many of the subsequent themes of the house are stencilled in a long, continuous sentence (3). The two main ideas are of cosmic time (the seasons, the passage of the sun, moon and galaxies) and cultural time (including Egypt, the Far East and India as well as Western civilisation). Above this a mural shows the evolution of the galaxies after the Big Bang, with, below it, a portrait frieze of a dozen paragons who symbolise for us open-mindedness: Emperor Hadrian, who brought Egypt, Persia and Greece into the Roman world; Erasmus, the freethinker; Prince Ito, who left Japan illegally to study Western ideas; through to Thomas Jefferson in conversation with Hannah Arendt. There is more meaning in William Stok's painting than this, just as there is more to the oval space fragmented into sections by reflections in mirrored doors, but both act as introductions to subsequent themes.

The first transformation of these themes occurs in the cloakroom and COSMIC LOO (a satire on all that has gone before). As in the COSMIC OVAL, the architectural order is emphasised by colour; light greys below, bright multi-colours in the middle and infinite cosmic gloom above, as in Westminster Cathedral. When one is bored with looking up at the heavenly kaleidoscope of mirrors overhead, one can play the 'postcard game' with a frieze of twenty-five postcards, three deep, that can be rearranged according to associations or preferences (4). Often loos have whimsical and personal ephemera on the walls, and I thought this might be given an architectural order reminiscent of Robert Adam's use of cheap paintings as a form of ceiling decoration. So the sub-Adamesque frieze celebrates our favourite buildings or the places from which friends have sent us postcards. This level is labelled *cosmopolite* (lover of the world), the ceiling *cosmos* (order of the world), and the mirror in front *cosmetic* (putting one's face in order, to face the world). There are fifteen other related words – including 'cosmotecture' (world envelope) – which may still find a place here. In every room we intend to add words and sayings which either pinpoint the theme or give it an odd twist. Unlike some Modern artists and architects, I don't believe a visual form is complete until it is given a caption, if only a mental one, as visual language is so often necessarily ambiguous.

The COSMIC LOO is a cul-de-sac off the COSMIC OVAL; the rest of the ground floor is given over to a sequence of rooms based on five seasons. These rooms, the most public area of the house, are organised around a central, spiral staircase and from any one of them there are views through into at least three others. The light-catching patches of space, reminiscent of a Dutch genre painting, are one of the effects we consciously sought throughout the planning of the house (5,6). Little vistas of domesticity are separately lit so the space seems to continue much further than it actually does. This idea is not so distant from the way space has been treated by Modern architects, which is perhaps why they find this aspect of the

3 The theme of windows on the world continues from the entrance into the WINTER and SPRING ROOMS. Window doors are used as storage units to create a smaller house within a house.

4 COSMIC LOO with its ovals, stencilled play on the paronyms of the cosmos and postcard frieze.

5   View from WINTER. Mirrors, arches, figures and furniture all order a complex open space with many elements competing for attention.

6   Samuel von Hoogstraten (1627-78) *Peep-Show Trompe l'Oeil* (detail) shows the tricks of light and perspective used to open up a house and dramatise a domestic scene. (Reproduced by courtesy of the Trustees, The National Gallery, London)

7   SUMMER ROOM, Allen Jones' *Summer* dances to the music of Father Time.

house the least displeasing. They are not usually fond of the way the seasons are symbolised.

The WINTER ROOM, in sombre colours, focuses on a fireplace designed by Michael Graves. He followed a symbolic programme based on the figure of Hephaestus, personification of Winter, above his forge – in this case the fire. Eduardo Paolozzi sat for Hephaestus and his bust, sculpted by Celia Scott, together with the colours of the chairs and rugs, is meant to convey a dark, wintry warmth, which contrasts with the colours and mood of SPRING next door. Here, the personification of the season is above another Michael Graves fireplace which, with the ceiling mirrors, again emphasises the cross-axis. My sister, Penny Jencks, made the bronze busts which symbolise April, May and June, or according to a traditional programme, Young Venus, Flora and the older (and wiser) *Venus Humanitas*. At points like this the eyes of some visitors begin to glaze as they wonder what possible relevance there can be in a Classical symbolic programme. My answer is that of the eclectic: 'As much as in the other aspects of the house – in the theories of science, or the epigrams of poets'. We haven't tried to give a single narrative to the house, or an overall world-view, but rather a synthetic historical view which mixes traditional and current meanings. Symbols are used as guidepoints rather than as points of dogma.

From SPRING we move clockwise into SUMMER (the dining room) then to INDIAN SUMMER (the kitchen) and finally to AUTUMN (a multi-use room). This opens onto WINTER and starts the cycle of time again. The Summer seasons are carved out of a single space which is divided by the built-in kitchen furniture and united by the warm yellows and pinks of the marble. Several conventional signs point to a place in time – the cornucopia painted on the floor signifies Summer, the mandala suggests India, and the grapes, maple leaf and chrysanthemum by the window are signs of Autumn.

Furniture and painting further emphasise the same themes. For instance, the SUMMER ROOM has as its focus six sun chairs around a circular sun table, with the nine planets running up the legs to culminate in a central burning globe which is represented also on the table top, on the balcony disc and even, in its colour, on the wall behind in Allen Jones' personification of Summer (7). In this painting she dances to the music of Father Time, clothed only in a warm, orange glow, while other rhythmical symbols (based on Poussin's *A Dance to the Music of Time*) surround her. Again the artist and I worked to a symbolic programme and, among other precedents, studied Poussin's painting and Panofsky's interpretation of it. In the same room, the sun's rays radiate overhead – geometric lines which start ultimately from the central staircase, the SOLAR STAIR. These rays, the actual floor joists, are then reiterated in the rays of the balcony structure and the fins of the vertical radiators. Lights over these transform the sun's actual heat and energy which come through the solar wall in front. So passive solar heating, real radiator heating and symbolic heat are all brought together in one elaborate equation of sign and symbol.

This combination of reality and representation can be found in every room. For instance in the kitchen (8), wooden salad servers are painted to resemble marble to form a decorative triglyph placed where you might find one in a Doric Temple: this 'spoonglyph' representing food, of course, is above the Temples to Heat (the oven) and Cold (the refrigerator). And so it goes: part practical symbol, part ridiculous sign, part aesthetic decision, part serious comment on the structure, space or material. ('A stirring mixture,' said one visitor, pausing by the spoons.) Whether the meaning is light-hearted or portentous is less important to me than the fact that it is worked through systematically, so that it becomes relevant architecturally.

This is most obvious in the SOLAR STAIR, a part of the house I worked out with Terry Farrell. In fact, the Terry Farrell Partnership was instrumental for three years in overseeing much of the construction work in the house and along with the craftsmen/carpenters Steve Agombar and John Longhurst helped to make many of the trickier details work. The stairway is very much the centre of the house both in function and as a sign, and we keep coming back to it literally and metaphorically. It has fifty-two steps (for the weeks in the year), each with seven divisions (for the days in the week) and a decorative disc portraying its month. When one looks up the centre to the light at the top – sign of energy and hope – the undulating rays of three different constructional elements drive home the sun metaphor. When one looks down to the darkness below, the opposite meanings are suggested and reinforced by Eduardo Paolozzi's mosaic *The Black Hole* (9). This mosaic draws in the spiral motion of the handrails, again a literal sign of time (spiral galaxies, DNA, cyclical motion) and a very efficient structural device. As in other parts of the house, we consulted engineers and astronomers – not mystics or astrologers.

It is absurd to draw a hard distinction between fact and fiction, especially in symbolic architecture, but one must pursue symbolism with a certain rigour for its inner logic to work. The themes must be limited in number and tied to inherent architectural themes of geometry and function. The ARCHITECTURAL LIBRARY, whose space was also worked out with Terry Farrell, illustrates this point (10). Its function is to hold my collection of history books, starting with a period I find most interesting, the Egyptian. These books sit below a pyramid gable, while beside them the books about the Greek and Roman periods are housed in Classical forms. And so it goes through the history of Western architecture up to the present, ending with three Post-Modern skyscrapers containing mostly literature about that movement and three Late-Modern slabs housing Modernist tomes. The style and shapes are all part of the same grammar used throughout the house – a Free-Style Classicism based on the constructional possibilities of wood.

Several historians, such as Sir John Summerson, have seen a hint of Mackintosh in the building, especially on the upper floors, but while this Glaswegian architect has influenced my understanding of ornament, he was not consciously my greatest inspiration in terms of style. Rather, the common language comes from using wood as a flat surface and then organising the volumes in part according to the Classical principles of axis, cross-axis, hierarchy, symmetry and primary geometrical form. What makes it *Free-Style* Classicism is the way these geometrical forms are broken and reinterpreted. For instance, in the library, the face motif is broken at its forehead – resulting in a very unclassical flat-top – and layered on its sides to reveal the actual complex structure. A Classical Revivalist would probably have used a regular form, hidden the structure and surrounded it with a moulding. But for Classicism to be a living language it must, I believe, be able to express the new discoveries of construction and structure – the SOLAR STAIR is, for example, a reinforced concrete cylinder with a two-way double-helix of steel and encasing concrete, brick and stucco. The construc-

8   INDIAN SUMMER has 'Hindu' Temples to Heat (the oven) and Cold (the refrigerator).

9   *The Black Hole* mosaic, by Eduardo Paolozzi.

10   Panorama of the ARCHITECTURAL LIBRARY shows the bookhouses which range, in style and content, from Early-Renaissance to Post-Modern.

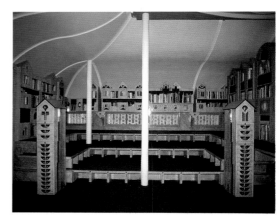

11 FOURSQUARE ROOM, the bedroom, uses the most ubiquitous motif in architecture in plan, on the ceiling and as decoration. The stencilled proverbs are also concerned with 'fourness'.

12 MOONWELL, a lightwell in the shape of a half-circle, like the moon, is reflected in a mirror to become a full one. The light globes are also reflected and at the top can be seen more images of the moon including the one etched on the mirror.

tion itself always provides a means of architectural expression. Other examples are the 'slide skyscrapers' which have a Classical base, shaft and crown, but with ornamental details which either emphasise the furniture's use ('M' for modern slides) or the actual steel construction.

The room most people find reminiscent of Mackintosh (and usually like the best) is the main bedroom, which we call the FOURSQUARE ROOM. I wouldn't argue with their evaluation, but again I believe the style and organisation owe as much to Free-Style Classicism and wood construction as to Mackintosh. Only the repeated violet foursquare pattern used as a frieze motif is consciously influenced by his work. Otherwise the creams, whites and off-whites of Adam's Syon House have been an influence, as well as the Palladian ABA motif and the ceilings of Sir John Soane and Frank Lloyd Wright. Symbolically, everything is based on the number four: the four cardinal points, four great civilisations, four elements (and one hundred and four of today), four ages of man, four parts of the day, and that most ubiquitous of architectural elements – the square (11). We inhabit a foursquare built world, although it could conceivably have been otherwise, with Buckminster Fuller's triangular geometry or African circles. But the number four resides in more manufactured or built objects than any other number. It is found in books, video-cassettes, automobiles, and almost every room and building you will use has four primary edges. I wanted a room in praise of this metaphysical phenomenon – ordered, of course, by the four-by-four inch wooden pier. Light and space filter into the bedroom from all four sides and vistas of the SOLAR STAIR, BATHPOOL or MOONWELL open up from it. These connections of space and light, insisted on by Maggie, give the room a special quality which changes throughout the day. If there is a single disadvantage to the semi-open plan, it is the old Modernist problem of sound transmission, although this is lessened by the fabrics and rugs.

There are many more thematic rooms in the house which are also designed to a symbolic programme, but perhaps they can all be symbolised by the MOONWELL (12). Designed partly in collaboration with others – Terry Farrell, Simon Sturgis, Maggie, and Ilinca Cantacuzino – the vertical shaft itself illustrates in part the theme of collaboration. But it is also unified by Free-Style Classicism and the symbolic programme. A half-moon plan is reflected by mirrors to form an entire globe and magically extend the space. Many people get lost in this part of the house (although it is quite modest in size) because of the spatial illusions. When one looks up, there is a mirror etching of the moon, based on close-up photographs, and a series of crescents and globes. The real moonlight can be reflected down this well and there are spots in the mirror where you can 'catch the moon'. Conceptually, the MOONWELL and SOLAR STAIR are satellite and globe. Atmospherically, the former casts a cool, silvery light down its thin shaft. Ornament, lighting, space, artwork and colour have all been directed towards the common theme not because we are moon worshippers – or I hope lunatics - but because symbolic architecture fulfils a desire. Of this I can be sure for a very simple reason. When I show sceptics around the house, they inevitably start 'reading' the building in ways I have not intended, finding plausible, new connections, extending the plot in unforeseen ways. Once they understand that the architecture has meaning, they expect to find more, and thereby discover new ones. The search for meaning in architecture, apparently, is as natural and desired as it is in life.

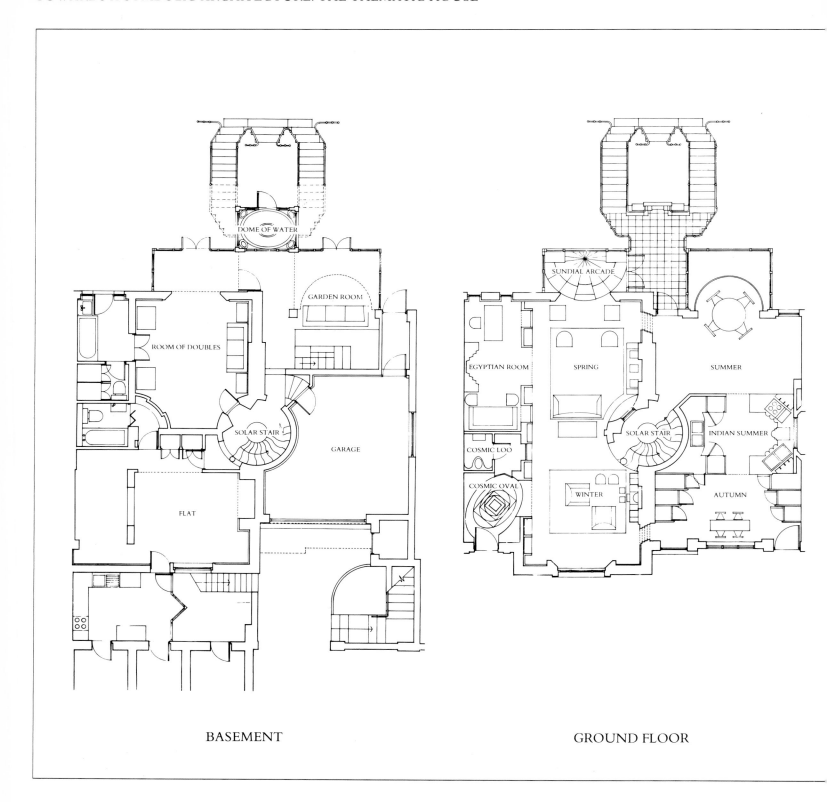

BASEMENT

GROUND FLOOR

1: THE PLANS

The existing four-storey house had its stairs inconveniently located on the south side. This interrupted views and cut out light, so we moved them to the centre. The house is divided roughly into four main areas: a basement given over to garden rooms and play rooms, a ground floor serving more public functions, a first floor which belongs to the parents and a top floor that the children occupy. Most of the pre-existing walls have remained, although many are cut through to allow light and space to suffuse the rooms. The fundamental structural change is the addition of the two conservatories on the south side to let in light and heat, and of the cylindrical staircase to hold up the side walls.

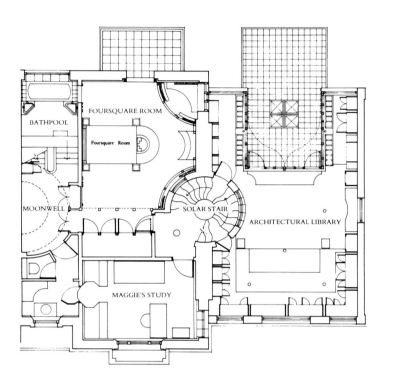

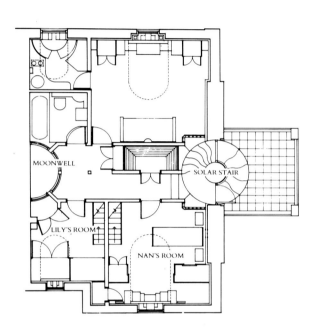

FIRST FLOOR   SECOND FLOOR

The central SOLAR STAIR of fifty-two steps unites all four floors; the MOONWELL opposite unites the top two. The basic rhythm of a terrace house is AB – that is a small bay for the entrance and stairs and a large one for the sitting rooms and bedrooms. We have kept this rhythm and on the ground floor mirrored it to make ABBA. Running the other way, north-south, is an implicit rhythm of ABA with the small central b generated by the sun and moon. Most of the rooms have demi-forms or fragmented Classical shapes; most are opened up spatially by vistas and at the same time closed or defined at their edge.

2: THE FACADES

The building as we inherited it was made up of a 1840s house at the end of a row of three, and a low studio and garage added in the 1950s. Neighbouring houses are in a similar vernacular style of London stock brick with cream stucco and trim. The balcony rails have a curious, sub-Mannerist motif we named 'rabbits', which we repeated in our new addition.

Basically we extended the grammar of the existing house, playing it fairly straight but becoming more personal at the rear. The two chimneys, London columns, are an abstraction of a sunburst breaking through clouds and relate to the tall neo-Classical chimneys directly across the garden. The arched face motif was used for the dormer windows to bring more light and space to the children's rooms, and was repeated in a different form under the steel pediment on the west facade. Here it has a double function: to pick up the theme of our neighbour's dormer windows and to introduce an anthropomorphic shape to inanimate form. Thus in several ways we have made the building fit in with its surroundings.

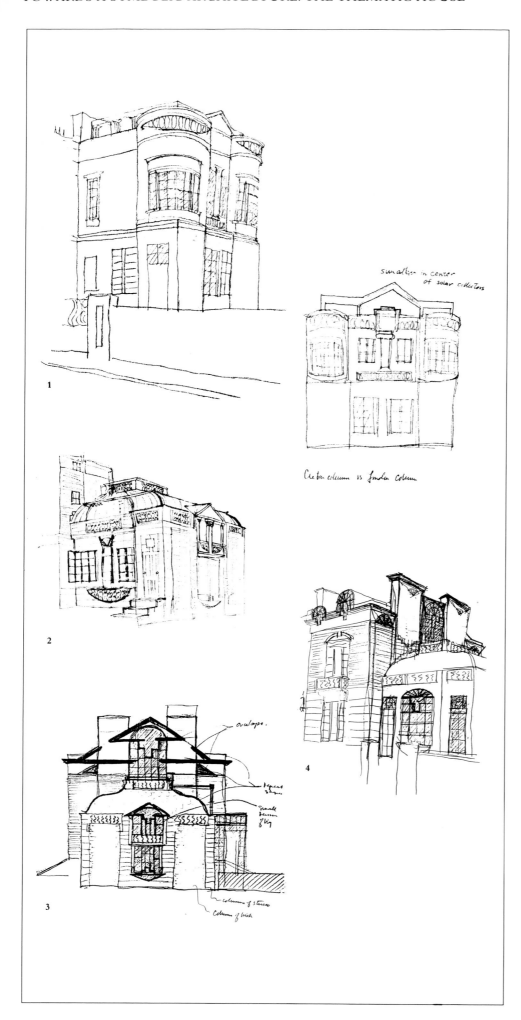

1

2

3

sun altar in center of solar collectors

Cretan column vs London column

oculops.

repeat form

small person & key

columns of stucco

columns of brick

4

DEVELOPMENT OF WEST FACADE

Some of my very first sketches for the house in June 1978 show several ideas that were eventually realised despite many transformations – notably, a central face on the west facade, the London column, the repetition of the 'rabbits', and the notion of a solar house. The first sketch (1) shows an abstraction of a face with a Cretan column played against a London column and a sun altar of solar collectors below an abstract pediment in metal. Terry Farrell thought planning permission for the addition of a full storey would be impossible and suggested a small addition with a straight-sided mansard roof. The second sketch shows my response – a version of a Hildebrandtian S-curved roof (2). The next stage involved an attempt to unify the chimneys by means of a giant broken pediment and to repeat this above the lower face (3). It was not until I thought of the chimneys as London columns, however, that we got near the final solution (4). If one counts the central stairway as a column of space, there are now five columns reading across the elevation. Terry Farrell and Simon Sturgis built a model of this drawing and worked out its complex spatial and structural implications.

One month later, in July 1980, I drew up the penultimate elevations and worked on reconciling all three facades, using axonometrics as well as individual studies (7). This was some two years and perhaps thirty or forty elevational drawings after the first rough sketches. The facade study reproduced here shows the final solutions to some of the complexities. First, the addition of the central stair column above the central face gave focus to the verticals on either side. These verticals are made from banks of stucco and brick, alternating ABACABA across the lower part of the facade and ABCBA across the upper, chimney level. The simplicity of this syncopated movement was a refreshing conclusion after so much complexity. Secondly, the central face motif and its awkward curve (necessary for practical reasons) were drawn together by a superincumbent pediment. Thirdly, the flaring London columns with their sunburst coming through the clouds became a unifying formal and symbolic device repeated more explicitly in the interior. Finally, the swelling S-curve of the roof ended here in stylised palms – a ridiculous symbol for London, but a sign to us that we needed some visual culmination to these flowing shapes.

This conclusion led to the next step: the idea that statuettes should be placed on the two plinths. I settled on the notion of personifying Art and Architecture and sent my sister Penny, who is a sculptress, some drawings, photographs and a thirty-page photo essay on personification in architecture, as well as a symbolic programme. Part of it reads as follows:

Personification of Art & Architecture
Architecture, mother of the arts, crowns the ogee curves to the roof and culminates the view to Summer and the garden. She turns towards her twin Art, now split from her, and beckons for a return to an impossible unity. She rotates on and through the essential element of architecture, the square/column/wall/podium giving life to this inanimate form. Her dress shows a dual nature: half workman's overalls, half a blousy shirt with rolled-back sleeves and ruffles . . . Between her and Art is a dividing barrier of indifference – the impersonal grid. A crack or fissure in the mythical unity of the arts and building trades, caused by the triumph of agnosticism in all areas, divides a curtain hung between them. They each pull their own way.

Art looks to the street life and the setting sun, on the diagonal. Her youth shows a fresh optimism and belief that anything is possible given the intention and right craft. Her dress shows a complex beauty . . . Her useful objects – brush, geometrical palette, scalpel, scroll, computer, iconographic book – are balanced by a concetto, the idea that should govern art. This 'concept of the concept' is represented by an openwork globe . . .

The allegory continues with a description of the divided art world broken up into its 'isms'. Whatever Penny made of this programme, she did come up with many solutions, two of which are shown here (5,6). One shows the figures engaged with the plinths, the other has *Art* (left) and *Architecture* (right) freestanding. The scale of the figures was kept small, both to avoid competition with the chimneys and to give the effect of distance between them. During the summer of 1981 Penny and I worked together on one or two more versions, but finally we abandoned the whole idea and she worked instead on personifications of Spring (see below). At some future date perhaps small symbolic urns (which have already been designed), will finally provide culmination for these natural points of visual force.

SYMBOLS AND GRIDS

The London columns have a flared void at the top, a sunburst through which one can sometimes see the sun (1). At their base is the stagger motif, which according to Egyptian and Greek convention symbolises earth. These signs are made more explicit in the interior London columns.

The pediment and 'rabbit' rails are made from a neutral steel grid, not only to signify Post-*Modernism* but also to tone down the facade (2). Some architects such as Denys Lasdun find the pediment too flimsy, but I wanted to indicate its non-structural role: it is supposed to take one's eye off the unfortunate relationship between the arch and roof curve which was forced upon us by building codes. The *trompe l'oeil* and metal grids below this transform the pediment's theme. The 'rabbit' frieze drops just below the face and two 'rabbits' are actually sliced to indicate their non-structural role.

On the entrance facade (5), dormer window faces indicate the children's rooms (3) while the front door face has all our initials (4). The original rustication of the stucco has been renewed and the garage door, which is prefabricated metal with a version of rustication, harmonises with it.

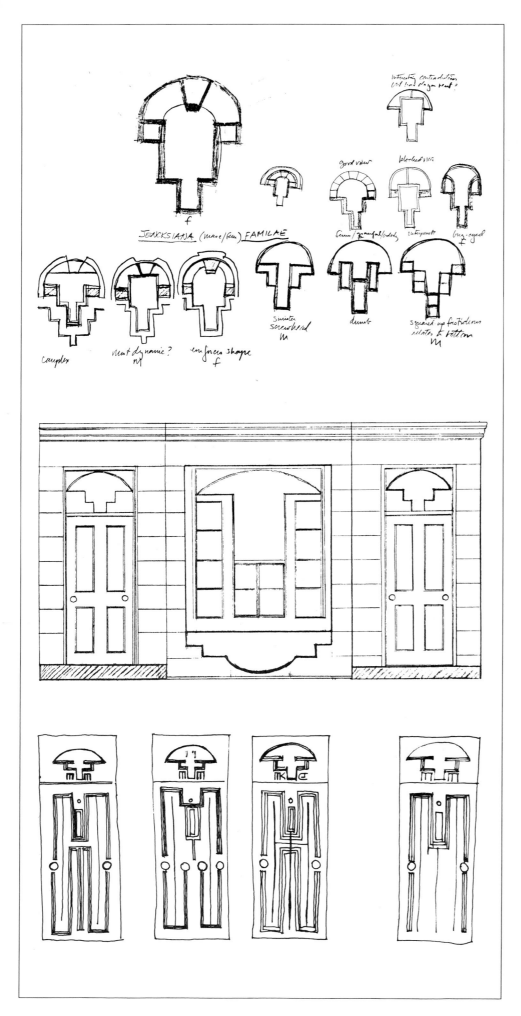

THE JENCKSIANA

Around 1975, I decided to develop a flexible motif of variable dimensions rather like the Serliana. The idea was that one form could be used in many guises – like an easily recognisable key word with both major meanings and minor overtones. In formulating this new motif, the Jencksiana, I was looking for a combination of feminine and masculine forms epitomised for me by the curve and the stagger. These were put together as a face, with the suggestion of a forehead, eyes and a chin, as in this early sketch (1979) for the house (1).

The motif can be expanded vertically or horizontally, with a change in function, and then the 'character and sex' are changed. Like the Palladiana with its flexible ABA rhythm, it can become very tall and thin. Since it is a figure, as opposed to background, it naturally takes one's eye off the mistakes in background rhythm which often occur when one is adding to an existing building. And since it is the abstract representation of a face – a suggestion rather than a literal rendition – one can empathise with the form. I had at the time been stressing in writings on anthropomorphic architecture that we naturally project bodily states onto buildings and this seemed a natural place to test the theory.

The entrance elevation of our addition has two body/doors on either side of an implicit face (2). The left one is false and opens out over space; it was included, like the double doorknobs, to maintain the symmetry and thus focus the eye on the central window. Although these doors never got their heads, the front door did (3). I worked through many versions in an attempt to reconcile function (doorknob, letter-box, fanlight, number and eye-hole) with the body image. At one point, we called the motif the Napoleana, a character which is quite evident here. The motif was then developed through more than thirty versions, some of which are shown here (4). Fat and dumb, pert and silly, owl-like and solemn, straight and balanced, cat-like and surprised – the cast of characters, if not a complete human comedy, is wide. The archetypal shape – the basic face as it were – is far left in the second row. The ugliest versions are in the fifth row. Perhaps with a computer one could fill out a complete set of physiological types.

REAR FACADE

For the rear elevation we used the same white stucco and brick as the surrounding buildings, but shifted the balance slightly towards the stucco (1). As a result, the facade is particularly sensitive to changes in the colour of the sky and the seasons. Four figures, crowned by face motifs, give focus to different parts of the building and garden. For instance the two conservatories – the mother and father if we read them literally – face the lawn with a dog, or monster, between them directly on the garden axis. In a conventional Palladian building, a grotto with a grimacing face might have occupied this position; we have abstracted the monster and combined his hair with the voussoirs so that the image is more subtle. From the conservatories, one's eye shifts upwards and to the right to the two dormer windows – the two children whose bodies are layered like birds. All this anthropomorphism is intended to be subliminal, so one can feel the presences rather than spot them immediately.

The stairway connecting the ground floor and the garden can be appreciated most clearly in the snow scene, in which incidental detail is edited out and the contrast of the industrial stair and rails with the Imperial, or double, staircase is more striking (2). The double stair obviously allows more movement, but its real *raison d'être* is psychological – it embraces the garden, and, as at so many châteaux, allows easy, enjoyable descent. Building a gracious staircase out of readymade, industrial parts was a particular pleasure.

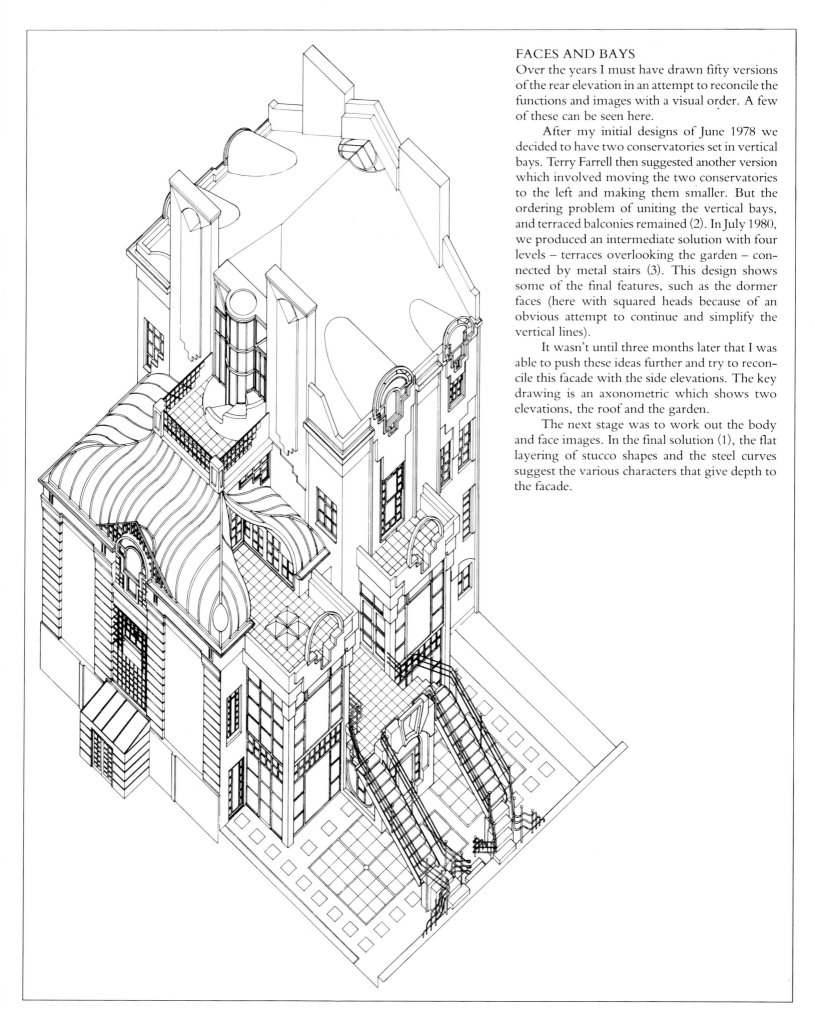

FACES AND BAYS

Over the years I must have drawn fifty versions of the rear elevation in an attempt to reconcile the functions and images with a visual order. A few of these can be seen here.

After my initial designs of June 1978 we decided to have two conservatories set in vertical bays. Terry Farrell then suggested another version which involved moving the two conservatories to the left and making them smaller. But the ordering problem of uniting the vertical bays, and terraced balconies remained (2). In July 1980, we produced an intermediate solution with four levels – terraces overlooking the garden – connected by metal stairs (3). This design shows some of the final features, such as the dormer faces (here with squared heads because of an obvious attempt to continue and simplify the vertical lines).

It wasn't until three months later that I was able to push these ideas further and try to reconcile this facade with the side elevations. The key drawing is an axonometric which shows two elevations, the roof and the garden.

The next stage was to work out the body and face images. In the final solution (1), the flat layering of stucco shapes and the steel curves suggest the various characters that give depth to the facade.

IC LAW IS   TIME'S RHYTHM WHICH   RULES SUN & MOON   THE FOUR SEASONS TOO   GIVING HEAT & LIGHT   OVER ALL ARCHITECTURE   EGYPT & CHINA BE

3: THE COSMIC OVAL

This entrance room is a broken oval which propels one into the main living rooms. Titled the COSMIC OVAL, it is designed to be pretentious – to pretend to more knowledge and wisdom than we can possibly have. Whether the world started as a Big Bang or Cosmic Egg, is Continuously Created or Oscillates, or even started Some Other Way – which is most likely – is allowed for by the iconography. Different readings have been planned, all based on currently plausible theories evolved through consulting astronomers and cosmologists and reading standard books on the subject. Although a certain interpretative licence was given the artist, William Stok, whose description of the work appears overleaf, Maggie and I wrote the initial programme and chose the two basic themes.

The first of these concerns the evolution of the cosmos from the Big Bang (over the front door) through the gradual development of the galaxies. The second focuses on a group of historical figures who for us symbolise open-mindedness, creativity, eclecticism and world exploration. We wanted a clear exposition of themes that wouldn't be merely illustrative and I think William Stok has struck the right balance between historical realism and abstraction.

The seventeen doors of the oval have the major themes of the house stencilled above them in a continuous sentence. The alphabet uses the curve and stagger of the Jencksiana; the letters are fragmented and were designed for their architectural presence rather than for their legibility. In some cases a single theme, such as the foursquare motif, has become the basis for the design of a whole room, while others, such as the windows on the world, reappear throughout the house.

COSMIC AND CULTURAL HISTORY

Several theories of the history of the universe contend that it began with a Big Bang – a theory which has affinities with the model favoured by previous cosmologies, the Cosmic Egg. The Big Bang is depicted in the COSMIC OVAL above the front door, which can also be seen as a White Hole – continuous creation – pouring out of a Black Hole from the 'Anti-Universe' (3). The blue band within the painting (read from left to right, as the oblique brush-strokes imply) shows the gradual evolution of matter into elliptical and spiral galaxies – 'Time's Rhythm' – which is also represented by the red band above. Below these levels are historical figures from different cultures engaged in conversation. For instance the Egyptian architect and physician, Imhotep, looks down at his stepped pyramid while Pythagoras looks up at the heavens to confirm his theory of number. The sequence ends with Thomas Jefferson and Hannah Arendt debating cultural revolutions which derive, etymologically, from cosmic ones (2). Rather than describing our original programme, we have reproduced here the artist William Stok's reinterpretation since it is obviously closer to the final result.

I based the structure of my work on the diagram of numbers drawn on the vase which the figure of Pythagoras holds in the painting. The diagram is a triangle, made up of nine signs arranged in four horizontal bands, which correspond to the basic mathematical numbers.

Number one, the top of the triangle, is represented in the hallway by the circle in the middle of the dome.

Number two, the second band, is represented by the division of the circle into two sections, yin and yang.

Number three, the third band, corresponds to my painting which is itself divided into three horizontal sections.

Number four, the fourth band, refers to the four walls of the hallway and also the sides of the quadrangle inside the ellipse on the floor, which represents the earth.

I selected one of the primary colours for each of the three lower bands of the painting – red, blue, and yellowish brown. This follows the conception of the celestial hierarchy formulated by Dionysius Exiguus in the fifth century. Red for the seraphim, those nearest to God, blue for the cherubim, angels and sky, and yellow for the earth.

In the first band the serpent with its undulating form contains a sign of the zodiac in each one of its twelve curves. The serpentine line attempts to imitate the flowing of the river, the god Oceanus.

In the second band the elliptic shape above the front door represents the Big Bang, and also echoes the Tantric Cosmic Egg, symbol of creation. I have used the ellipse because it is an integral part of the design of the house, for example in the dome in the hall and the drawn ellipse on the floor. The elliptic shape refers to Kepler's discovery of the shape of the earth's path round

the sun, and it can also be found in the structure of the atom. I imagined the elliptic shape in the atom as a representation of the microcosm, with respect to the elliptic shape of the earth's circumvolution, parabola of a comet, or shape of a galaxy, the macrocosm. This band represents the beginning of the world after the Big Bang and the inclined, parallel brushstrokes, which become darker as they move away from the light source, signify the growth of the cosmos from the first elements in creation, helium and hydrogen. The galaxies formed from the cosmos are depicted around the walls and they return to the ultimate collapse of matter in the universe, the Black Hole.

In the third band twelve eminent historical figures are depicted. In cosmology the number twelve stands for the macrocosm and I intended my work to be linked with the cosmos, not the earth. The figures are not shown in full, but just to the waist, like the sculpted busts in the two rooms adjoining the entrance. Each person is represented by a sign, a 'hieroglyphic' with a symbolic meaning which unites the figures.

Imhotep has the sign of the ziggurat to represent the fact that he was the first architect in Egypt to create a building made in stepped form. The ziggurat was built in imitation of sacred mountains; it was called the mountain of god or the heel of heaven. It was composed of seven steps – seven was thought of as the number of perfection, a sacred number. Imhotep is connected to the next figure, Pythagoras. They both made use of mathematics, the Egyptian for functional reasons and the Greek for abstract or metaphysical reasons. Both Imhotep and Pythagoras were adulated as god-like figures after their deaths.

Pythagoras has the diagram he designed which consists of the first nine numbers. Once again this is in the shape of a ziggurat.

The Chinese Poet *holds an ampulla in the shape of a pagoda. This is the symbol of divinity and its central column is the centre of the universe. The sign the poet is represented by is the lotus flower. The lotus was originally a symbol of the sun in ancient Egypt, then a symbol of the continual renewal of life. It still had the same significance when it migrated to India, and thence to China and Japan.*

Hadrian *has the sign of the Pantheon which was built under his rule. The dome of the Pantheon represents the cosmos and the 'eye' in the dome is the sun. The four walls of the interior under the dome each have a sculpture – representing the four seasons.*

Abbot Suger *rebuilt St Denis in the reign of Louis VII. He holds an eagle with the sign of the fleur-de-lys on it, the emblem of the French monarchy and symbol of life. The symbol of the eagle is explained under Erasmus, the next figure. It is relevant to Abbot Suger as he spent much time speculating on the metaphysics of light and it was said that 'everything that shone stimulated him'.*

Erasmus, *translator of the New Testament, is shown reading a book with an eagle on it. The eagle is a Christian symbol of ascension because of its powerful upward flight, with 'its gaze fixed on the sun'.*

The Jesuit Astrologer *holds an astrolabe. On it is a symbol of wisdom, the serpent, which I have drawn eating its own tail to represent eternity, adapting it to the theme of my work.*

John Donne, *the metaphysical poet, is given the sign of the broken column (the support of life being broken) as in the Renaissance era this meant death, a recurrent theme in his work. Death, specifically the skull, together with a book (which he is holding) was a symbol of time.*

Borromini *was the architect of S. Ivo della Sapienza. Here he is drawn next to its pinnacle, which is divided into seven parts to create another ziggurat. The spiral symbol of growth is drawn onto the pinnacle emphasising its twining shape.*

Prince Hito *is wearing the sign of the chrysanthemum, the national flower of Japan and a favourite of the Japanese Emperors for many centuries.*

Thomas Jefferson *has a vase at his side which comes from the Roman 'Maison Carrée' at Nîmes. The plan of the University of Virginia is drawn on it. In designing the University, Jefferson conceived a central Pantheon-like rotunda with colonnades linking small temple-like pavilions.*

Hannah Arendt *is holding a papyrus scroll of the Jewish laws. I visualised her in this way because one of her books is titled 'Between Past and Future' and a scroll is generally used as a symbol of life and time, with the inscription on one side of it representing the past, and the inscription on the other the future.*

On one side of the projecting corner is the sun with the emblem of the crow, on the other the moon with a three-legged toad – a figure from Chinese legend. At the base of the loggia is a vase with the sign for water, symbol of regeneration. Sprouting from the vase is a twig, the tree of life and knowledge.

I don't expect everyone looking at the symbols to understand their significance, because that would require a certain amount of research. However, I find the signs illustrating the symbols intriguing in themselves; mysterious, as for example, Egyptian hieroglyphics or Arabic and Chinese characters are to those who do not know their significance. The viewer is invited to take part in the slow process of reading the painting and the fact that some objects held by the figures and names inscribed on

the wall can only by seen in their entire form from certain viewpoints increases the difficulty of grasping the whole meaning immediately.

I did not try to make portraits, in the sense of reproducing the exact physiognomy of each person. I used photographs or else used people to whom I am related as though they were actors. I tried to give a different 'skin' to people that I know so that I felt closer to the work that I was making. I used my brother as a model for John Donne and Pythagoras; Roger Kennedy, a psychiatrist friend, for Hadrian; and Pat Moynihan for Abbot Suger. The face of the Jesuit astronomer was based on Luciano, one of my students. Hannah Arendt came from my grandmother and the 'putti', my daughter, Christiana.

I used the pinnacle of S. Ivo as the sign for Borromini as it is the church in which I was married. The Pantheon, sign for Hadrian, is the building which my wife insists on visiting every time we go to Rome.

One sign of the zodiac – my own, the sign of Aquarius – is hidden by the loggia. I felt this was a way of putting my signature.

I thought it was important to dedicate the work to the owners of the house and for this reason I incorporated the signs of the zodiac as drawn by Charles Jencks. I also drew the signs for the figures in the same way as hieroglyphics, where the outlines are of a different colour. I did this as I was aware of Charles Jencks' interest in Egyptian art. For Maggie Keswick I chose two symbols, the moon and the sun, part of Chinese mythology, which fascinates her.

William Stok – December 1984

111

THE JENCKS TYPE-FACE
The stencilled sentence describing the major themes of the house uses the Jencks Type-Face, based on the curve and stagger of the Jencksiana. The sentence reads: *'THE COSMIC LAW IS/TIME'S RHYTHM WHICH/RULES SUN & MOON/THE FOUR SEASONS TOO/GIVING HEAT & LIGHT/OVER ALL*

ARCHITECTURE/EGYPT & CHINA BEGIN/ARCHETYPES & READYMADES/THE FOURSQUARE MOTIF/WINDOWS ON THE WORLD/THE 5 BUILDING ARTS/IN FREE-CLASSIC STYLE/TWENTY-TWO FACES/AN ECLECTIC WHOLE/OF PERSONAL SIGNS/OWLS, LILIES, CATS/FIX A PLACE IN TIME.'

abccddefghijkk

lmnopqrsstou

vwxyyz zo

&?!e$o.,:

pe$o

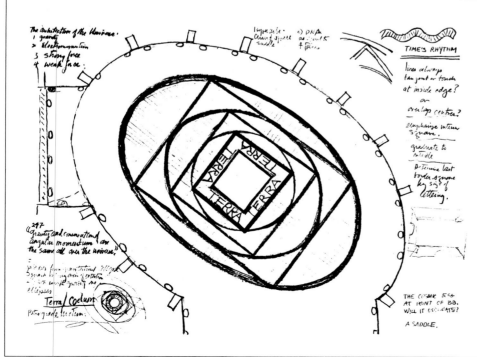

EARTH AND SKY

In most cultures the circle represents the sky and the square the earth. We have used this symbolism within the COSMIC OVAL and in places translated it into intermediate forms – rectangles inscribed in ovals. For example, the central Terra sign on the soft-wood floor is an inlaid mahogany square (1,2), while the centre of the ceiling dome is a mirrored circle (3). The vertical layering of the space is again a version of traditional usage: colourful and complex shapes are near the base and abstract and simple ones are near the dome (4). This usage continues into the COSMIC LOO and cloakroom, forming a semantic system which connects the three rooms. The system is also continued into the living rooms. The windows on the world continue down one side, while above this level are busts and space for future paintings. The mirrored ceilings relate to the dome taken at its most abstract level: purity, simplicity and thought.

The oval dome and its mirror-image on

the floor are based in part on Guarino Guarini's openwork domes of the seventeenth century which were also reflected in plan, at least in his drawings. The openwork structure allows light to spill through in mysterious ways and implies infinite movement, a concept being formulated in Guarini's time and one which he apparently wished to represent.

Before proceeding with the painting, William Stok made some cartoons which we discussed with him. The process took several small models, two or three sheets of full-scale sketches, then egg tempera painting in a studio and finally repainting on site.

Since the COSMIC OVAL is an introduction to the themes of the house, it had to be visually ordered and simplified – hence the repetitive windows on the world used as a decorative order. Most of them open to store things – umbrellas and light bulbs – but two work as a door into the cloakroom and parody of all this pretension, the COSMIC LOO.

4: THE COSMIC LOO AND CLOAKROOM

In the COSMIC LOO both the symbolic content and form of the COSMIC OVAL are transformed. While ovals in the entrance ascend in concentric rings towards the sky, in the COSMIC LOO they descend towards the earthly loo seat. White globes and abstract shapes maintain the cosmic pretensions; these are located, as in the oval, above a more colourful level – provided here by postcards of our favourite cities and landscapes, or places we or friends have visited. The postcard frieze sits below a moulding labelled *cosmopolite* (lover of the world). Above this, to the left, is the root word *cosmos*.

To the Greeks, for example Pythagoras, *cosmos,* as a system generated by numbers, was in opposition to *chaos*. The word has come to signify the order, beauty and harmony of the universe and has produced numerous paronyms. For example there is *cosmometry* which means 'measurement of the universe' and *cosmology* which means 'science or theory of the universe as an ordered whole' (1656). A *cosmian* is a 'secular person of the world' (1842), a *cosmophile* is a 'lover of all countries in the world' (1882). *Cosmolatry* means 'worship of the world' so our recent *cosmonaut* should really mean 'ex-lover of the world who has transferred his affections to the universe'. *Cosmotecture* means 'world envelope' (1624), although architects might think otherwise, and a *cosmocrat* is a 'Lord of the World'. There are many more derivatives, one of which is *cosmetic* 'having the power to adorn or beautify' (1658) which we placed next to the mirror: putting one's face in order to face the world's order. This strange linguistic relation between the universe and the face has always fascinated me.

Thus the *cosmos* is the top level which is dark, blue and abstract; *cosmetic* is the mirror level; and *cosmopolite* is the lowest, most colourful level. We intend to add further sayings: 'I cannot believe that God plays dice with the cosmos' (Albert Einstein) or 'The cosmos is about the smallest hole that a man can hide his head in' (G. K. Chesterton).

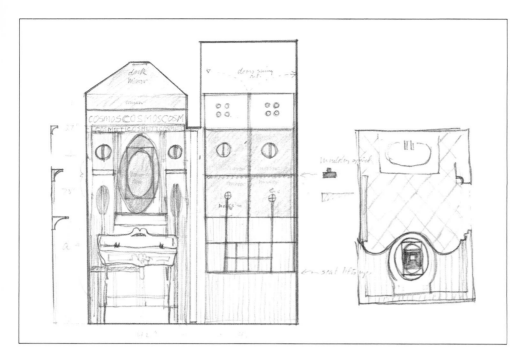

THE KALEIDOSCOPE

Typically one enters a house through a vestibule, removes one's coat in a cloakroom and 'washes one's hands' in a euphemism. We have dramatised this ritual by introducing themes at the entrance – doorknobs, windows and dark mirrors – which culminate in the ceiling above the loo, the kaleidoscope (4). This, with its geometrical *white* extract fan at the top, can inspire interesting speculations on the nature of the universe. Usually, the Black Hole is considered the ultimate cosmic sink.

Doorknobs are used in the cloakroom as hooks and a coatrack (2). A grid of mouldings and mirrors unites the storage for hats (above, with 'planetary' holes for ventilation) with that for boots (below). The main light globes (suns) are common to the cloakroom and the loo – where they are also treated as eyes in a face (3). Ovals and doorbolts are also given fillets of mirror as a reflective infill.

5: THE WINTER ROOM

The Winter Room is the first of the seasonal rooms on the ground floor and it faces north. One thus enters the house at the beginning of the year, in January as it were, and, by walking through the rooms around the Solar Stair, can complete a full cycle of seasons. The walls are painted in shades of grey and the rugs and furniture are in warm but sombre reds and greens. A major decision was Maggie's idea of painting the floor dark aquamarine blue, less to signify Winter than to unify the Winter and Spring Rooms. The semi-opaque stain just allows the wood grain to show through, something we wanted since the knots and swirls resemble suns and galaxies. But from a distance, several layers of polyurethane gloss give great reflective depth to the colour, making it rather like polished marble. The conventional picture of Winter is of an elderly gentleman wrapped in rug-like shawls huddled by a fire reading a book. Thus old age, warmth, saturated colours and reading are traditionally associated with the coldest season. These signs and functions are further epitomised in the bust of Hephaestus and, on the mantelpiece and table, by the Chinese rocks which resemble fire and represent, among other things, age.

LIGHT AND SUGGESTION

Dutch genre painting of the seventeenth century captured an ambiguous quality within domestic life which is perhaps most apparent to children. The interiors are full of foreboding shapes, over-large furniture and objects of uncertain use, set against a clear, 'rational' light. Whether the cheerful light or mysterious gloom predominates depends on the observer.

Emanuel de Witte's *Interior with a Woman at a Clavichord* (2), for instance, shows an apparently innocent scene of music and household chores. Good, clean Protestant light rakes in from one side, defining the rooms and the edges of the treasured objects within. It is only on close inspection that the meanings of the darker elements are revealed: the tell-tale jug of wine, the black clothes and sword thrown over a chair and then, peering out of the four-poster, the barely visible face of the lover.

Emanuel de Witte *Interior with a Woman at a Clavichord*, c. 1665 (Reproduced courtesy of The Netherlands Office of Fine Art)

WINTER

We have tried to reproduce something of these qualities of light and suggestion by opening up the house so that small vistas are revealed. From several spots one can see into four different spaces, each with its own quality of light (1). One can imagine from the photographs a different set of characters in each space, all up to their typical activity: the elderly gossiping in WINTER about the lovers just visible in SPRING, and so forth. Here, however, there are only two very heavy chairs, portly gentlemen, conferring with two Biedermeiers. The former are heavy because they are made from MDF (medium-density fibreboard), which is painted in *trompe l'oeil* with a wood grain that elaborates the theme of cosmic activity (3). What appear to be fibrous swirls and knots are in fact representations of nebulae and stars (4). The advantages of MDF are its sharp finish, low cost and ease in layering which allows much of the furniture to include echelons, or staggered profiles. Pyramids and obelisks are set into the niches. The furniture is conceived as architecture in miniature to restore a presence to everyday objects.

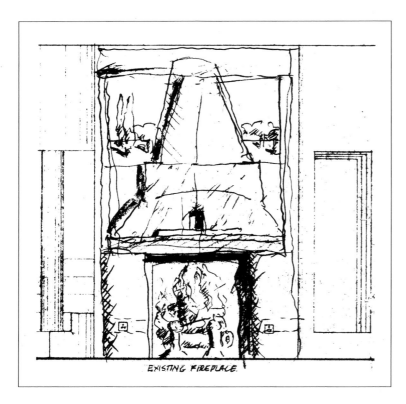

EXISTING FIREPLACE.

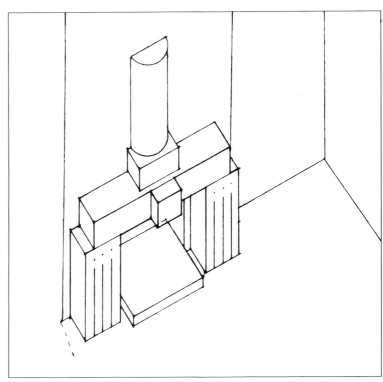

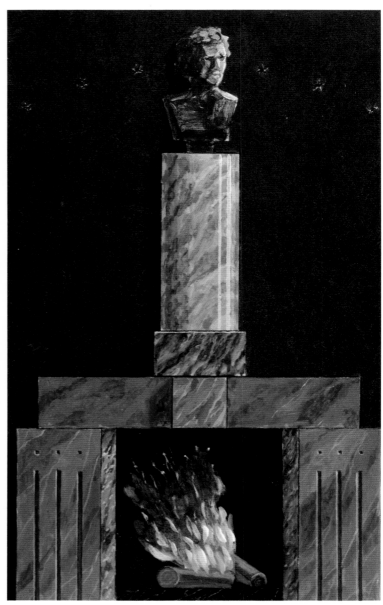

HEPHAESTUS

Hephaestus, in classical mythology the smith at his forge, has often been used to symbolise Winter (6). His name in Greek derives from the words meaning 'hearth' and 'to kindle' and his presence over the fireplace thus has a triple motivation: it is his forge, the hearth of the house and a place to go in Winter.

We gave the designer of the fireplace, Michael Graves, and the sculptor, Celia Scott, quite an elaborate programme, which described Hephaestus as a 'robust smith, with bearded face, powerful neck and hairy chest'. Eduardo Paolozzi consented to sit for the bust (5); the beard and zodiac signs for January, February and March were added for the final casting (7). Paolozzi, himself among other things a sculptor in metal, a teacher and a friend well-known for his generosity, thus stares out over our heads as an embodiment of strength and beneficence, the Winter god who gave civilisation metalwork and man the mechanical arts.

As one would expect, Michael Graves has interpreted the programme on a monumental scale. His solution is a basic post and lintel structure carrying an engaged column (2). The fire, or forge, is framed by the fluted sides and massive red lintel (again made from MDF but now painted to resemble marble). We have placed two tiny chairs in front of the fireplace, symbolically for Hephaestus' helpers and aesthetically to contrast with the gigantic chairs in the room. Graves' first sketch was for an extremely heavy structure, made up of cylinders, with small paintings on either side of a central cone (1). The final version has the same contrasts of volume (3), but now in different (though all dark) marbles (4).

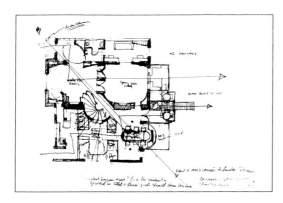

OPEN AND CLOSED

There are two basic spatial notions on the ground floor: the idea of the shifted axis which leads one, as in a Parisian hôtel, by stages to the garden, and the idea of a diagonal axis with a focus on opposite corners. The wide-angle view shows the way one's eye is pulled towards the central stair on the diagonal (3). This is a strong focal point because of the bright colours and the daylight spilling in from the dining room and conservatory. The longitudinal axis, reinforced by the book storage, or the theme of windows on the world, provides just as strong a pull (4). Here the repetition of grey glass windows and double doorknobs is a welcome contrast to the complex colours and meanings. I conceived this wall as leading the eye in a simple perspective zoom to the garden, framed by two columns.

A sketch plan made in 1979 shows many of our final ideas (1). The entrance oval leads onto the diagonal axis – in contrast with the two axes that shift towards the garden stairs. Sunrays penetrate from the central stairs into different rooms, setting up staggers that are taken up in the wall thicknesses. The cloakroom and loo are shown almost in their final resting place (2), but the gentle curves of the mouldings and the doors between WINTER and SPRING have gone. The final plan maintains the mixture of open and closed space, Modern and Classical organisation, visible in the first.

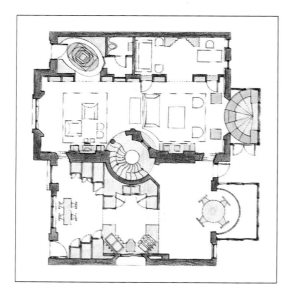

6: THE SPRING ROOM

In the SPRING ROOM, en suite with WINTER, slight changes in both colour and theme are introduced. There is a lighter tone of grey on the walls and ceiling, lighter rugs, here with floral patterns, and honey-coloured furniture. But the mirrored ceiling and lighting system continue to focus on the major axis moving to the garden and the minor axis centring on the fireplace and arch. A shell motif, a traditional symbol of Spring, is repeated in the furniture, fabric and two columns of light – the London columns. A floral motif, another conventional symbol, is stencilled on the fireplace wall. The central personification of Flora, above the fireplace, gives this idea a human dimension.

The Spring sofa, with its windows on the world, stands in front of the EGYPTIAN ROOM, which can be seen through further windows: its shell arch is a flattened version of the arch in the background. These photographs were taken at night when the lighting is cool and flat, but during the day when the sunlight streams through the conservatory windows the whole room takes on a more golden hue, giving a much greater feeling of Spring.

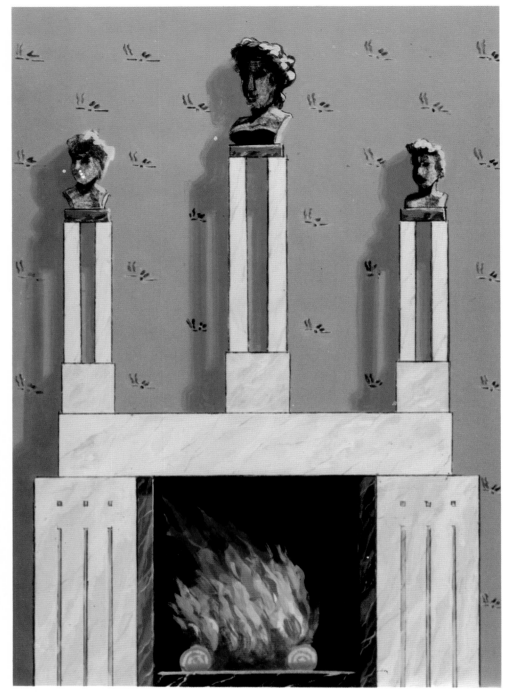

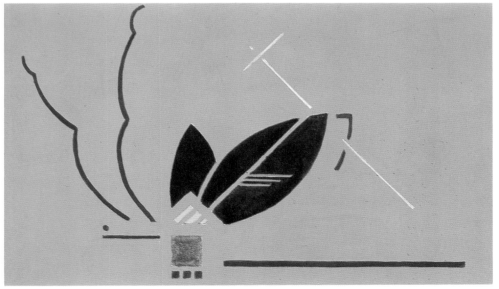

SPRING FIREPLACE

The design of the Spring fireplace went through several stages. First we asked our friend Rem Koolhaas to design it, but he rather over-extended the brief to the whole wall. Then we saw Michael Graves' designs for the Winter fireplace and realised that one designer had to do both since they would be seen together. Thus Graves' final version is a transformation of his Winter fireplace. It has the same base, minus the masculine protrusion, and three sets of thin, feminine pillars instead of the massive half-column (1). Although the symbolic programme specified a background of flowers, the stencilled pattern looks to me more like a lot of Constructivist bugs playing polo (2). The result is very pleasing, however, and also very Spring-like.

My sister Penny Jencks made the bronze busts that symbolise April, May and June. Friends furnished the models. Early Spring was posed for by Cressida Hare while Marcia Hare, her mother, was the model for Late Spring (3). Flora Phillips provided the model for Mid Spring, or Flora. The programme I sent Penny was fairly detailed and it is gratifying to see how many of our requirements she met while giving, at the same time, a twist to our interpretations.

Sculptural programme for the Spring fireplace
The ideas to be expressed by the three figures have to do with the notions of rebirth and pleasure through light and sunlight, and the two aspects of Venus – love and humanitas.
Early Spring, April, is a young passionate girl in her fresh vigour, full of laughter with just a touch of sarcasm which irreverent youth brings. She looks to Flora and Late Spring in anticipation of future enjoyment. This will be based on enlightenment and art. She, the passionate Venus, the inspiration behind Spring's energy, has a sign of April, the ram's head, stylised on either side of her shoulders – where the arms would have been. In the background early Spring flowers are painted on an open meadow.
Mid Spring, May, Flora, is not only the goddess of budding, but here also the symbol of the extraordinary London May: the burst of sun through the usual overcast grey. Her hair, slightly like a sunburst, slightly punkish, symbolises ecstatic enlightenment. She looks straight across the room with eyes that could penetrate a wall. On either side of her is a stylised sign of May, and behind her plants grow up either side of the shaft.
Late Spring, June, looks wiser, more pensive, naturally a time-worn version of April, but just as beautiful. She can resemble, loosely, Botticelli's central Venus Humanitas, the expression of refinement and culture. She has the Gemini sign redesigned where her arms would be, and in the background full Summer foliage.
Thus the allegory is of the transformation from Early to Mid to Late Spring, as the sweetening of culture. Culture is here taken more in the vegetable and physical than the moral sense, although enlightenment is involved. The allegory is also of the two Venuses – physical and refined love overseen by Spring light. All of this is to have a contemporary look and not smack of the bookworm.‡

‡ Bookworms will want to consult E. H. Gombrich's interpretation of Botticelli's Primavera, *reprinted in* Symbolic Images, *London, 1972, pp. 36-62.*

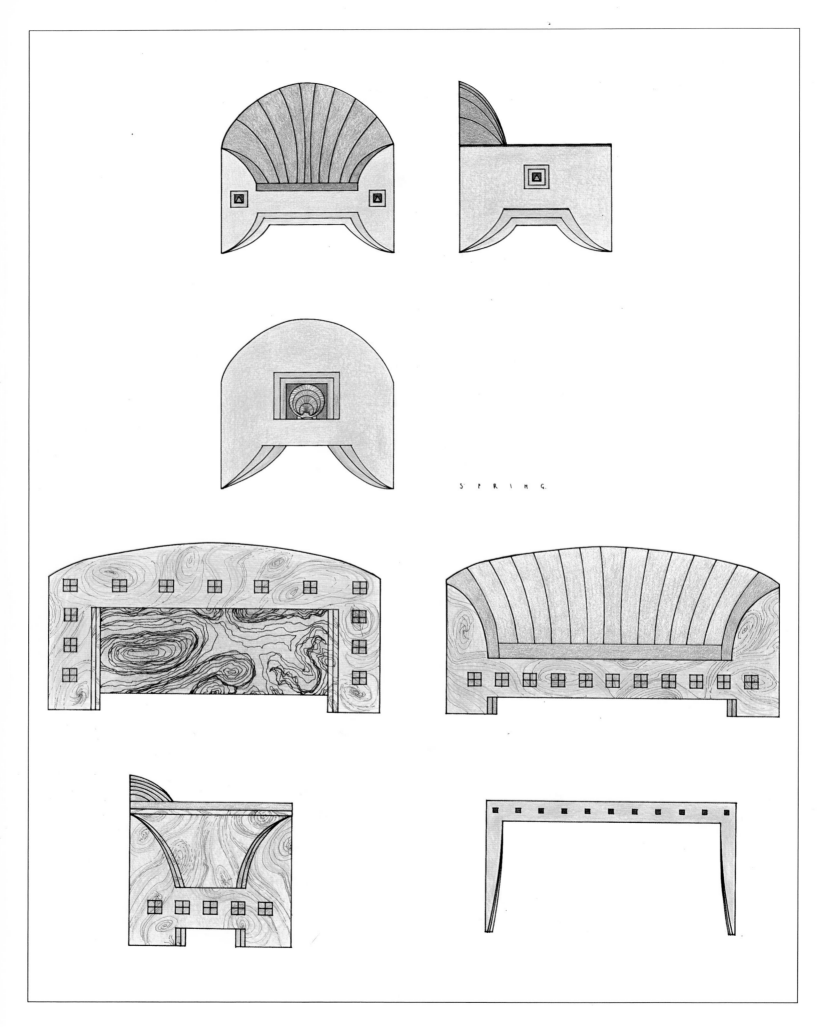

SPRING

SPRING FURNITURE

The SPRING ROOM furniture varies in colour from a light honey-colour to a yellowish satinwood. It is constructed, like the WINTER ROOM furniture, from MDF and thus features the echelons, sunbursts and shell motifs which can easily be formed with this material (1).

On the Spring sofa are decorative windows on the world which once again reveal nebulae and fire storms in their graining. On the sofa back, the curtain pulls aside, as it were, to reveal darker cosmic activity beneath the stage arch. At one time the windows of this sofa were to contain stylised trees and flowers, but these were not included in the final version as they would have complicated the reading of the cosmos. The top of the sofa has a soft shell-like curve and the sides have trumpet shapes, or fans of echelons, like the Summer chairs.

These trumpet shapes are turned upside down at the base of the Spring chair. Inlaid on the sides and front are onyx pyramids bought in Egypt for about one dollar each. The idea of using 'readymades' in furniture occurred to me when I saw how beautiful and cheap these pyramids were, and since Egypt was already one of the themes of the house, it was a happy confirmation to find the virtues of prefabrication still practised there. The shell set into the back of the chair is also a readymade, this time a Wedgwood plate costing about seven dollars which has been re-painted to fit the Spring context. I think the echelons are more effective in this chair than in the rest of the furniture because there is an implied continuity, especially at the back.

The six dice table/seats have the same windows looking onto more cosmic wood grain. Their central sections are triglyphs and while top and bottom are exactly the same in each one, the moulding profiles of the bases and crowns graduate from one to six.

In the distance can be seen one part of the EGYPTIAN ROOM and its *Ka* (spirit) wall which hides various pipes (3). I shrank this door motif and put two eye lights overhead to recall one of the elements of Egyptian architecture, the false wall through which the departed looks back at the world he has left (2).

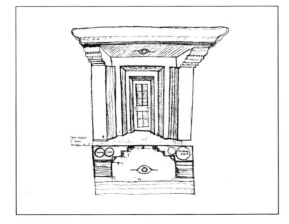

LONDON COLUMNS

The columns which form chimneys on the west facade also appear in modified form inside the house. As in Classical architecture, the order progresses in terms of delicacy and detail from outside to inside.

The columns in the SPRING ROOM have prefabricated shell lights as part of their capitals; they also contain bookcases in their shafts and hi-fi speakers in their bases. Both exterior and interior columns are thus functional in new ways, although neither actually holds up anything except the sky – symbolised on the inside of the house by the mirror on the ceiling (3).

The columns inside the house are made from prefabricated mouldings turned sideways and two interlocking, flaring forms reminiscent of the Egyptian capitals which inspired them. The proportions were changed during construction for circumstantial reasons and the balance of sky, rain and clouds is less satisfactory than it was in the earliest sketches (1,2). Later computer studies, made with William Mitchell's group at UCLA, revealed even more grotesque alternatives and interesting meanings: 'uptight, pinstripe, zootsuit, Art Deco and crushed' are some of the overtones (4-9). A change in proportion, as Classicists said, is a change not only in style but also significance. Computer manipulation of the variables allows one to speculate quickly and treat such things as the intercolumniations as positive voids. In one instance, a horse's face was sought (7).

Why sunburst columns? In London, as they say, everybody talks about the weather but no one does anything about it; here at least we have used passive solar heating which comes through the specially treated glass just behind the columns. This part of the house, with the sundial arcade, is given over to observing the weather.

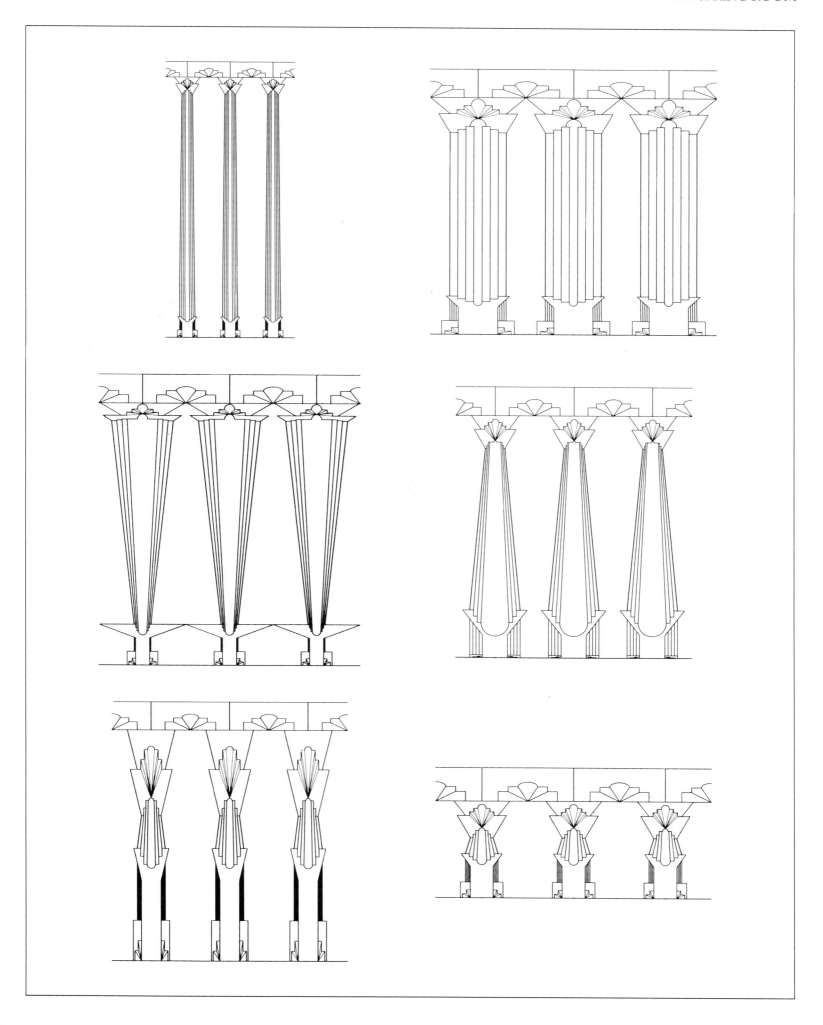

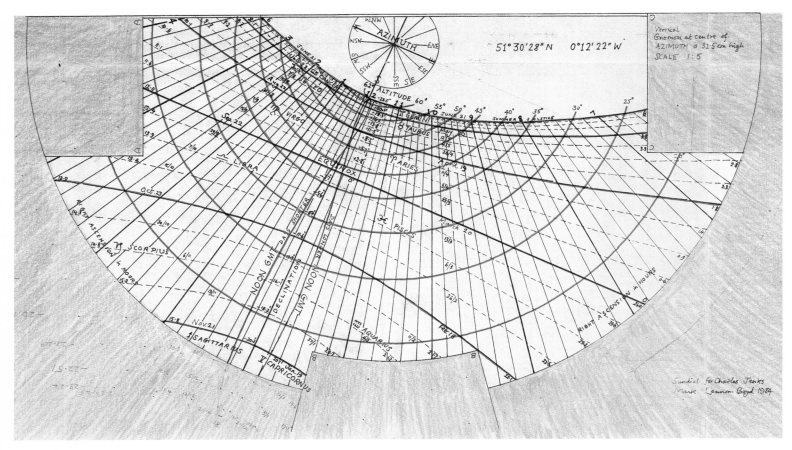

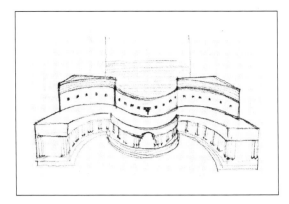

SUNDIAL ARCADE

This window seat, overlooking the garden, contains four different meanings. Looked at from above, the image is that of an arch, or face motif, with voussoirs of fabric to sit on and a dropped keystone, painted as stone, to step on (2). Looked at from the garden balcony, it resembles both an arcade and a set of terraces with small attic windows (5). This was the angle from which I conceived it, first as something akin to ancient Roman prototypes (3) and then later as the arched Jencksiana of its final form (4). The idea was to merge the functions of sitting, standing and leaning with the image of a recognisable building type to create an ambiguity or architectural pun. The final meaning is that of a sundial, an appropriate one since the space faces south against a solar wall. Mark Lennox-Boyd worked out the crucial scales with great precision, using a computer to calculate several cosmic measurements (1). These have yet to be painted on the floor, but the existing model works.

We hope the space will be one of the nicest in the house, when it is finished and has plants, curtains and cushions. Maggie initially conceived of it as a stepped-down window seat in close proximity to the garden. The whole window can be lowered electronically, allowing one to sit virtually outside.

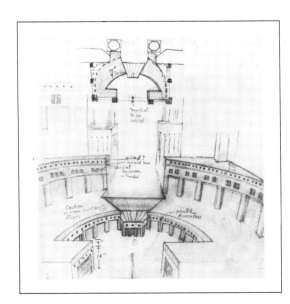

Photo: Ianthe Ruthven

7: THE SUMMER ROOM

The SUMMER ROOM, facing south, is painted in warm colours to recall the rays of the sun. These rays were often feared as 'murderous' by the Egyptians and Greeks; the name for the sun god Apollo, for instance, was derived from a Greek word meaning 'to repel', 'to destroy'. He shoots his murderous 'arrows from afar' and these rays are symbolised in the SUMMER ROOM by the ceiling beams overhead and the flare of the diadem arch. To either side of this arch, with its Horus disc – an abstraction of the sun – are flutes surmounted by light sconces in the shape and colour of a quarter sun. Apollo and Helios were also, of course, beneficent gods who brought forth crops and fruit – hence the cornucopia painted on the floor, another conventional sign of Summer. Four plastic pyramid skylights allow the sun to fall on this emblem.

EXPANDABLE SUN TABLE

The sun table and chairs were designed on the theme of Summer. The table's surface decoration focuses on a central, flame-coloured disc, the colours and forms of which are derived from close-up photographs of the sun which show it to be a violent, orange mass of flares and explosions rather than a peaceful white globe. We used the latter image below the table top surrounding another solar symbol – a round ball that acts as the marker for the table legs (1). The nine planets are painted on both sides of each leg, increasing in size towards the central focus. The wood grain is painted to resemble cosmic elements – swirls of nebulae and spiral galaxies – as an early sketch shows (2).

Incised black lines echo the sunbursts of the chairbacks and show on the edge of the table the edge of the universe where space and time are supposed to warp back on themselves. The expandable table is like the expanding universe.

On a practical level, four pull-out supports allow different additions to the table. The small version seats six to eight (3); the large one, with four leaves added, ten to fourteen (4). The additions are painted to complete the fan shapes of the table top.

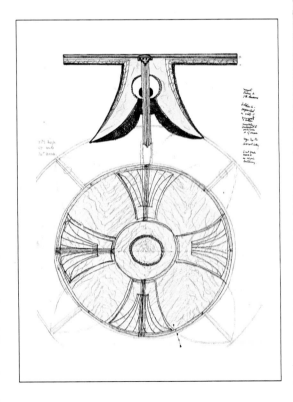

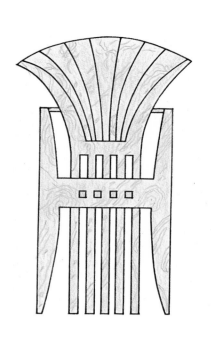
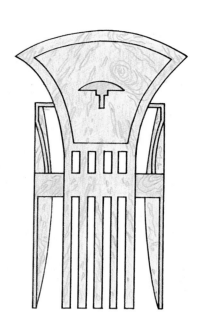

SUN CHAIR

The sun chairs and table were designed as a set made from the same MDF. In spite of the sunburst backs and hard–looking curved seats, the chairs are surprisingly comfortable since they follow the body's curves. Arms were added (1,3) to the

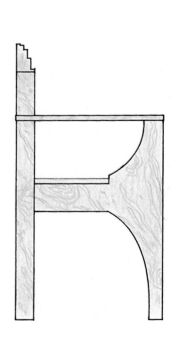

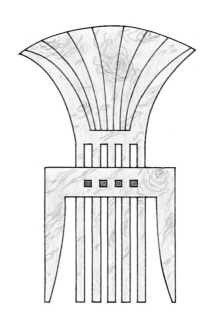

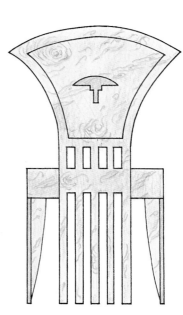

initial design (2) and there is a slightly better proportioned armless version (4-6). Both versions show the 'combs' of the back legs extending their lines of force into the sunburst which ends in a curve that is pleasant to lean on when turning in conversation.

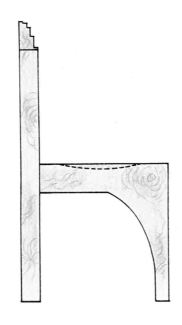

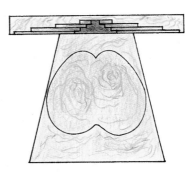

Nicolas Poussin (1595–1665) *A Dance to the Music of Time* (Reproduced by permission of the Trustees, The Wallace Collection, London)

SUMMER PAINTING

Allen Jones' painting *Summer* is based partly on Nicolas Poussin's *A Dance to the Music of Time* (4). As in the Poussin painting, Jones' Summer, a glowing dancer with a sheaf of corn, is watched over by Father Time who plays an instrument, while to the left, the Janus-faced herm looks to the new and old years (3). The glowing figure of Summer contrasts with the cool green used for the ageing musician isolated in a tree: these contrasts of theme and colour are also extended to the frame which echoes elements of the room such as the lighting and heat columns (1,2). The presence and strong colours of the painting provide a very pleasing contrast to the overall harmony, and one's eyes turn there continually. Erwin Panofsky's iconographic analysis of the Poussin painting in his essay on Father Time provided the impetus for the initial programme and also inspired the artist.

149

WINDOW WALL

The transition from SUMMER to INDIAN SUMMER (the kitchen) is made gently by means of *trompe l'oeil* terra cotta floor tiles. These create a cross-axis which moves through the house from one space to the next interspersed with emblems of the seasons painted on the floor. Dining room and kitchen can be divided by pulling out a row of mirrored doors. These reflect the views of the garden seen through the windows opposite and thus create a double version of one of the basic themes of the house – windows on the world. The mirror windows are between two other sets of windows, one real, the other decorative – that turn into INDIAN SUMMER.

8: INDIAN SUMMER AND AUTUMN

INDIAN SUMMER, the kitchen, and AUTUMN, the pantry, bring our cycle of seasons to a close. By wandering through both, and then through a door cut on a stagger back into WINTER, one can make a revolution around the central SOLAR STAIR – walk, as it were, through a solar year. The idea of designing the kitchen on the theme of Hindu architecture came, obviously, from the awful pun inherent in 'Indian' building and 'Indian' Summer, and less obviously, from my love of the former. Hindu architecture can be regarded as one of the great architectural traditions, like the Greek and Roman from which it may have developed. Speculations on this possible evolution – made after a trip to look at the unbelievably heavy columns of the caves of Ajanta – were incorporated into the design.

The squat columns, possibly evolved from the Doric order, have primitive flutes and are very good for storage. Behind the spring-release doors are pots, pans, coffee mugs and herbs. The three large columns under the gas hobs slide out and the eight paired and engaged columns above open as double doors. The idea of making an efficient kitchen in a more interesting style than fitted pine or High-Tech formica is achieved through the *trompe l'oeil* of most surfaces – floor, walls, counters and also some of the beams. Real marble surfaces sit above false marble (and unfortunately do not work as well as the *trompe l'oeil* versions, because they chip and stain). Johnny Grey and Mark Lewis did the working drawings based on many sketches and detailed discussions, and a team of painters – which included Sheila Sartin, Adrian Everitt, Valentine Abbott and Edgar Sirs – worked on this room and on AUTUMN. The great advantage of using *trompe l'oeil* is that it enabled us to avoid the countless functional and economic problems which would have resulted from using real tile, marble or stone and at the same time to achieve an aesthetic and symbolic order in what is usually an anonymous space.

SYMBOL AND FUNCTION

The first drawings for this space show a mixture of Hindu and Mogul architecture, chosen for functional reasons (2). For instance the characteristic hat-shape of a Mogul dome is used as an extract hood to remove kitchen smells, while the chunky stepped forms which are inspired by, and fit into, the stepped section, are for storage. A Hindu column is characteristically divided by subtracting geometrical sections. Here there is a progression upwards from the foursquare base of four:eight:sixteen:thirty-two.

On later drawings other ideas are added, for instance the light pink marble colour, inspired by New Delhi; the use of windows on the world to mirror the real windows above; the double Jencksiana in plan; and the sign of Autumn – some women carrying baskets of grapes on their heads (5). The grapes are related to the vines painted on the floor.

Many drawings, some full-scale, were made to resolve the frieze and capitals. The Greeks stylised wooden beams and featured them as triglyphs; we painted wooden spoons to resemble marble and featured them as 'spoonglyphs' – to symbolise the pleasures of eating. They form a three to two rhythm in a frieze above the Temples to Heat and Cold – the oven on the right, and the refrigerator on the left (1). They also alternate with voided metopes containing teapots (3). On either side of the central face motif are two Indian statuettes in peaceful poses of beneficence, while lower right is Ganesh with his many hands, one of which appears to be holding fruit. In the stylised details of each abacus one can just discern the difference between heat and cold, fire and ice.

Some of the plans show an attempt to resolve the slight contradiction of the central axis (inherited as part of the original studio) which doesn't quite align the windows opposite and has the asymmetry of the kitchen to cope with: here is an example of how the Jencksiana can resolve difficulties (4). Also apparent are the emblems of the seasons at the centre of each space, while diagonal axes of movement are taken up in the diagonal steps and chequers which also reflect the stepped section of Autumn. I think these drawings show more clearly than others the closed yet open style, the axial yet diagonal movement: the Free-Style Classicism.

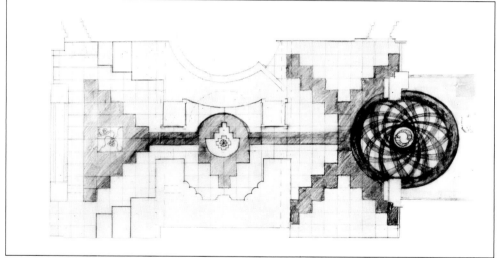

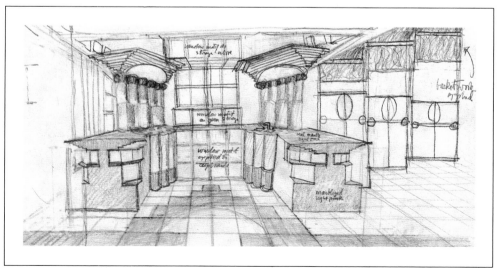

AUTUMN

The ceiling steps up from the kitchen towards the window to accommodate terraces of seating in the ARCHITECTURAL LIBRARY overhead and to relieve the oppressively low kitchen height (1). These steps are echoed in the tiles painted on the floor and the storage units (2). Containing food, wine and a trash-compactor on one side and a washing machine, dryer and utility store in symmetrical units opposite, these rectangles incorporate several signs of Autumn.

First is the mottled burnt red, a darker version of the hues of INDIAN SUMMER which are also echoed in the curtains. Second are the double doorknobs – the arms of the *ankh* signs and symbols of femininity. In perspective, the decoration is meant to suggest three women carrying baskets of grapes on their heads, a conventional image of Autumn, but here abstracted so that the meaning is not clear at first. Only when real or marble grapes are put into the voids above their heads – baskets of space which are only just visible (3) – will this image become more explicit. The forms were seen at their most abstract under the two coats of eggshell white which preceded the final *trompe l'oeil*. Again we took advantage of *trompe l'oeil* to reconcile conflicting geometries and meanings in a space which here opens into two other rooms – with a lot going on in all of them.

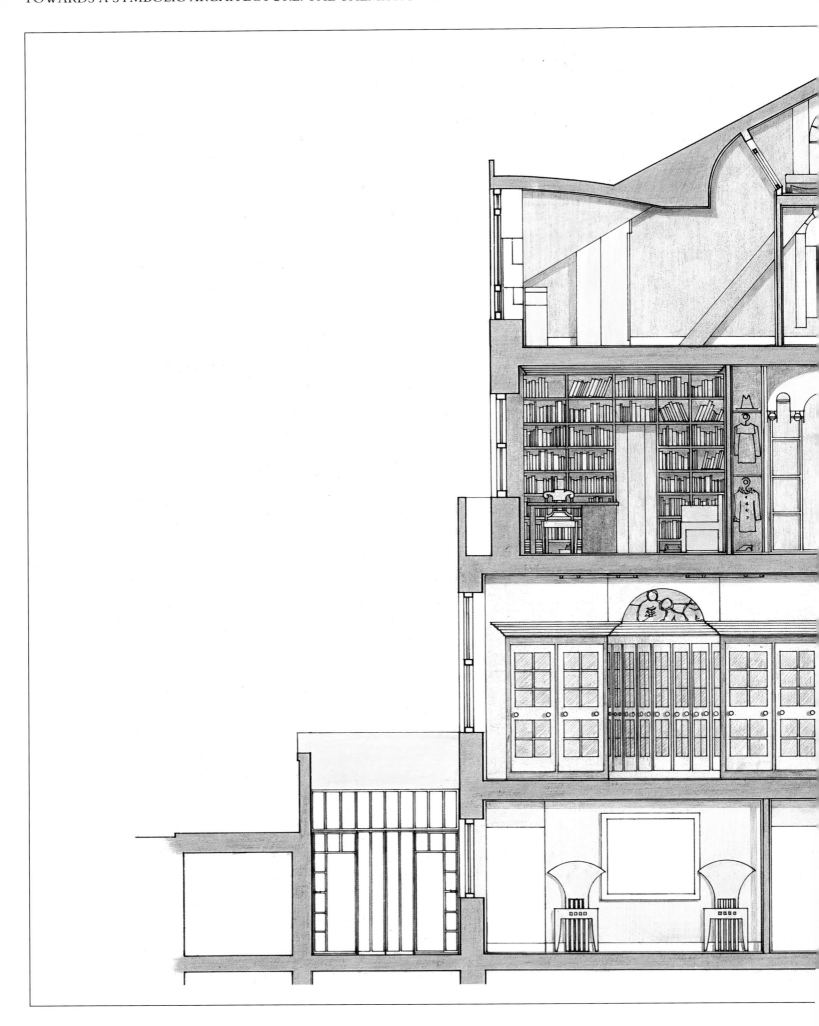

9: THE SOLAR STAIR

The SOLAR STAIR is both the physical and psychological centre of the house. One is constantly drawn here, both to use the stair, and to see across it from one room to another. From one spot five rooms, or rather small parts of them, can be seen in a single vista. We cut small windows or doors wherever structurally possible to create such vignettes.

The stair is an abstract representation of the solar year. It has forty-eight steps plus two at either end to make fifty-two, each of which is cast with seven divisions to give 365 grooves, one for each day of the year. Looking up, one sees the pulsations created by the shapes of the three different pre-cast stair units, culminating in a white disc. Looking down, one sees the undulating treads of each step. Since the stair is a spiral and the spiral a natural sign of time and motion through time (the whirlpool galaxies), we decided to ask Eduardo Paolozzi to design a mosaic for the bottom of the stairwell to represent such galaxies – *The Black Hole*. The lines of this mosaic, which Paolozzi worked on with Ray Watson, take up the curved lines of the adjacent concrete forms. In addition to the spirals are other images of time such as clockwheels. With the light dome at the top and the dark mosaic at the bottom, the resultant imagery is somewhat traditional in that light, energy and hope are associated with climbing up, and darkness with descent.

One can walk around the stair on the ground floor through five seasons and revolve, as it were, through a single year. Down the centre of the stair revolve three rails – representing the sun, earth and moon – which follow a spiral path through space.

DESIGN AND CONSTRUCTION

From the moment we decided to put a spiral stair in the centre of the house, I conceived of it as a representation of the sun. I had been lecturing on the stair as a type and was acquainted with Bramante's curving spiral at the Belvedere, Vignola's at Caprarola and Leonardo's strange construction at Chambord – all of which struck me as being natural metaphors of the sun, because the spirals end in a disc of light. Maggie and I also went to look at Inigo Jones' staircase at the Queen's House in Greenwich, which had evolved from these Renaissance models.

Terry Farrell, who was working on the structural integration of the stair with the surrounding cylinder, produced in collaboration with the engineer David French a system that would not only be self-supporting, but could also act as a column to hold up the adjacent chimneys. The system of construction they devised was supported initially by a tree of scaffolding.

Maggie and I started to study the expressive potential of the underside of the stair treads, inspired by Inigo Jones' Queen's House stair (3). An idea which would have been almost impossible for Renaissance stone builders arose: that of making the underside of the treads different. By constructing an extra mould we could make the fan-shaped ribs flare in different ways. I worked on several clay models, sculpting the undersides to give two contrasting types, and then doubly curving the tops so they undulated. Thus we had a double image of the sun, the S-curved rays on the top and the rhythmical fans below (4).

David Quigley, a designer in Farrell's office, counted the stairs and found there were fifty-two in all. This suggested the possibility of grooving each face seven times to create 365 divisions. Thus the structure and symbolic programme developed hand in hand. The compressed section shows how the stair unifies the two parts of the house – the original block and the 1950s addition (2).

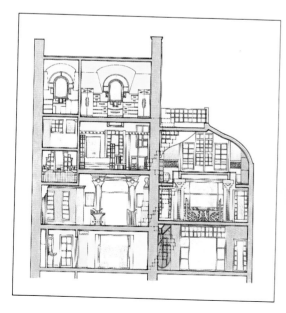

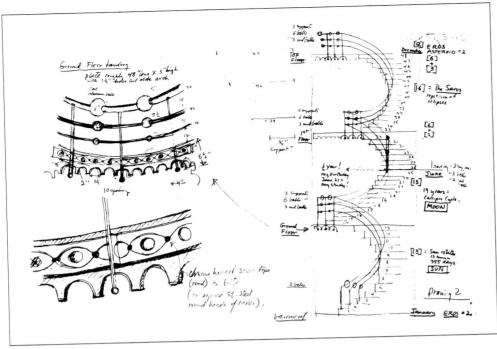

THE STAIR RAIL AND TIME'S RHYTHM

It took a considerable amount of time to resolve the technical and symbolic difficulties of the stair rail. The technical problem of the steep, curved pitch was ultimately solved brilliantly by the craftsman Colin Sullivan and his team. The symbolic problems concerned how to justify the position of the landings and the joints between concrete and stainless steel.

I settled on a system which started with January at the bottom and ended with December at the top, with four steps to a month and each month represented by a new version of the zodiac etched on mirror (2,3). This device neatly plugged the holes left by the constructional scaffolding tree. The stair rail was more complicated. If the biggest, six-inch ball was the sun, the four-inch one the earth and the two-inch one the moon, then what could be the significance of the vertical struts needed to connect them with the curved landings? All I could imagine were the small bodies – asteroids and comets – that fly occasionally through the solar system, so the struts have tiny polished balls at their ends. This still left the stainless steel fixing plate in need of meaning and form. Since it had to be screwed into the concrete, I worked out a system of chrome-headed screws connected by engraved sine curves surrounding voided circles – curves which repeat those of the COSMIC OVAL and are there referred to as 'TIME'S RHYTHM' (4).

Lastly, the major division of landings occurred at odd numerical points, the significance of which eluded me. So I consulted Dr McNally, an astronomer at the Royal Observatory, on this and other points concerning the possible astronomical meanings of the house. For this situation he came up with the following parallels. The first and last sets of two steps signify the period of the asteroid Eros; the first set of thirteen steps signifies the number of times the sun rotates in a year; the next set of nineteen refers to the Callipic cycle of the moon rocking in its orbit; the last set of sixteen refers to the Saros, or a repetition of lunar eclipses (1). So the meanings stay within the orbit of the solar system.

The half-landing, where the ARCHITECTURAL LIBRARY is situated, occurs fortunately about halfway through the solar year, about June 21st, which is my birthday – a happy coincidence.

10: THE MOONWELL

The MOONWELL is a shaft of space which cuts through the building to bring light to an otherwise dark landing and dressing room. It is on axis with the SOLAR STAIR, to which it is connected by a passage. Its mirrored surfaces create an ambiguity which many people find confusing. At first the space appears to be a cylinder, like the SOLAR STAIR, with a perfect circle of globes. Close up, however, it is recognisable as a half-circle in plan, with half-moons or crescents above. The surfaces are both simple and complex; the eye flickers over them trying to work out the paradoxes created by the mirrors and the repeated semi-circles and white mullions, which flare up or down. At the top one can see a moon etched in the glass which reveals, if studied closely, two figures from Chinese legend – the immortal tenth-century politician Liu Hai and his three-legged toad. Designed with Ilinca Cantacuzino, this is both a continuation of the theme of China and an homage to Maggie's father, John Keswick, who made a collection of three-legged toads and usually carried a small one in his pocket.

The eight globes and phases of the moon.

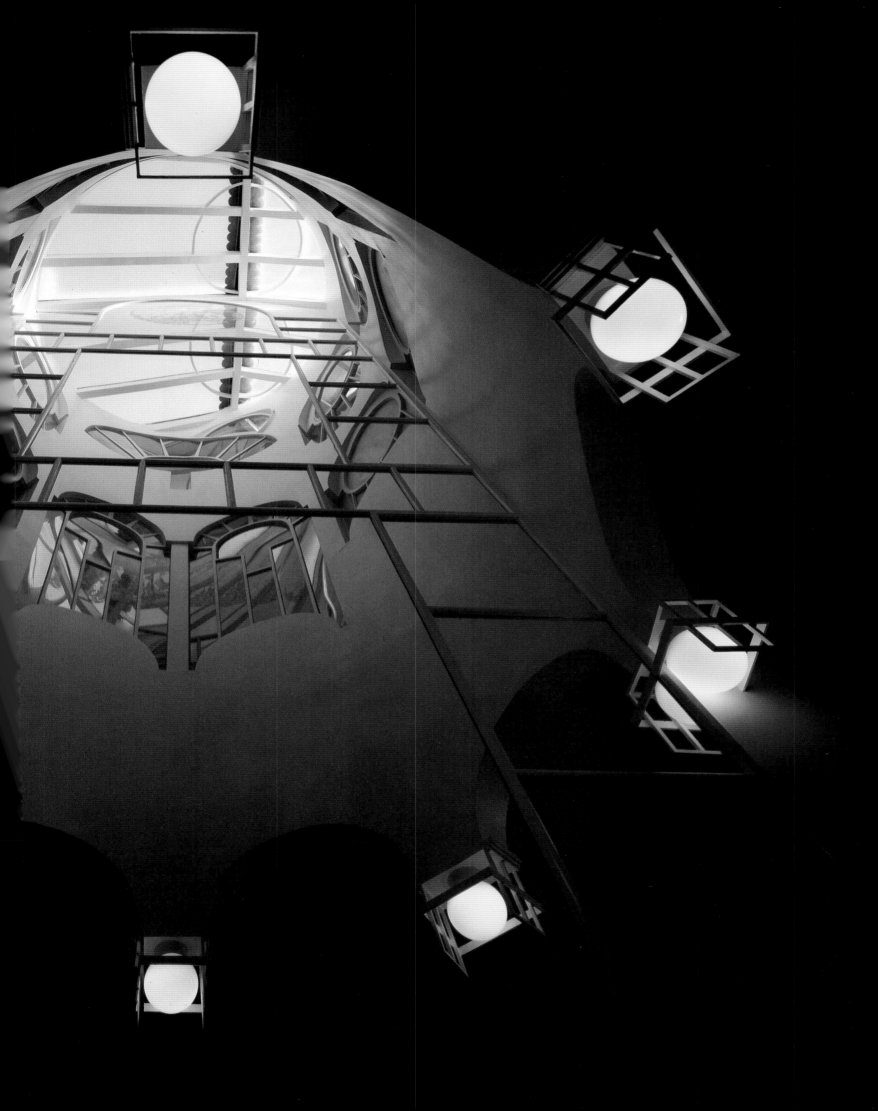

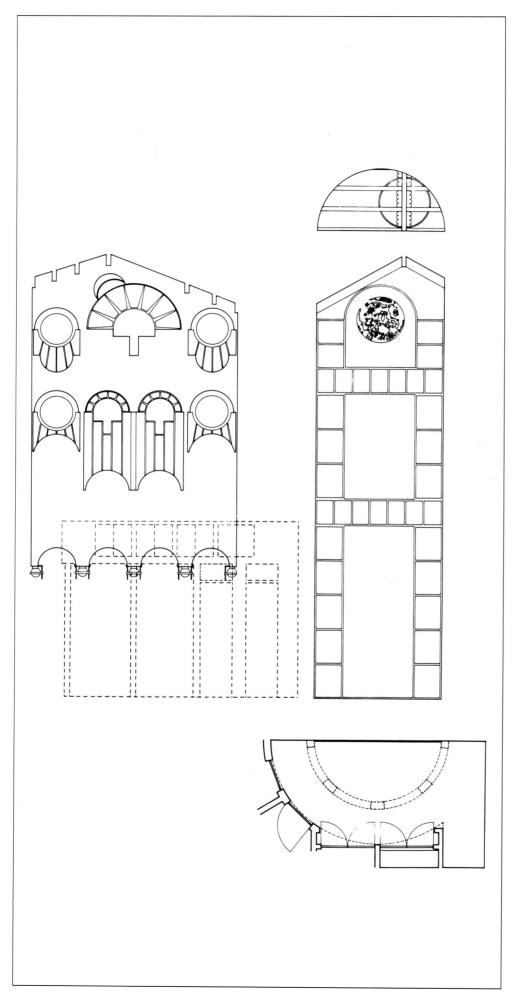

ABSTRACT REPRESENTATIONS

The first drawings for the MOONWELL had a column of mirrors flaring out at the top as in the London column chimneys. On further investigation, we discovered an asymmetrically placed ridge beam and so I designed a wall of mirrors that resembles the exterior conservatories. Simon Sturgis and I then worked on the window arches and crescent windows. At one stage I envisaged descending moonrays based on Egyptian representations and a man-in-the-moon crossed with a solar flare. Some of these ideas were included in the final design, but in a more abstract form (1).

We were always concerned with the fine balance between abstraction and representation and in Ilinca Cantacuzino's third version of the moon, etched in glass, the figures which are combined with the realistic images of the moon are barely visible (3). The Chinese man-in-the-moon is Liu Hai, with his three-legged toad (2). According to legend, the toad was avaricious and could only be winkled out of his hiding place in a well if Liu Hai fished for him with five gold coins: hence the two are traditionally symbols of good fortune. In the etching Liu Hai's eyes and hair are combined with moon craters, and the toad and his coins with lunar seas, thus giving several possible readings and a quite pleasing ambiguity.

11: THE ARCHITECTURAL LIBRARY

This room is made up of a village of bookcases set beneath a blue, curved ceiling and is supposed to recall the London skyline at dusk. Each of the individual 'buildings', or bookhouses, has a pitched roof to give an overall unity but is otherwise in a style appropriate to the subject of the books contained within it. Thus the volumes on Egyptian architecture are housed in pyramidal and proto-Doric forms, those on Roman architecture in a domical shape, Early-Medieval in stepped gables and so on, up to the asymmetrically pitched slabs of Late-Modernism. Naturally there is a problem: a library expands and so may never fit perfectly in the spaces. The fit here works well for about half the bookcases, where my collection is moderately balanced, but at points such as the Late-Medieval case, hardly at all. The under-filled cases hold magazines and books on non-Western architecture, which would otherwise have no place. Whether or not the fit between form and content is perfect is not the point: the idea is to make the usually neutral bookshelves tell a story. After all, if a village of houses tells us something about its inhabitants, why can't individual bookshelves convey something about the content of their occupants?

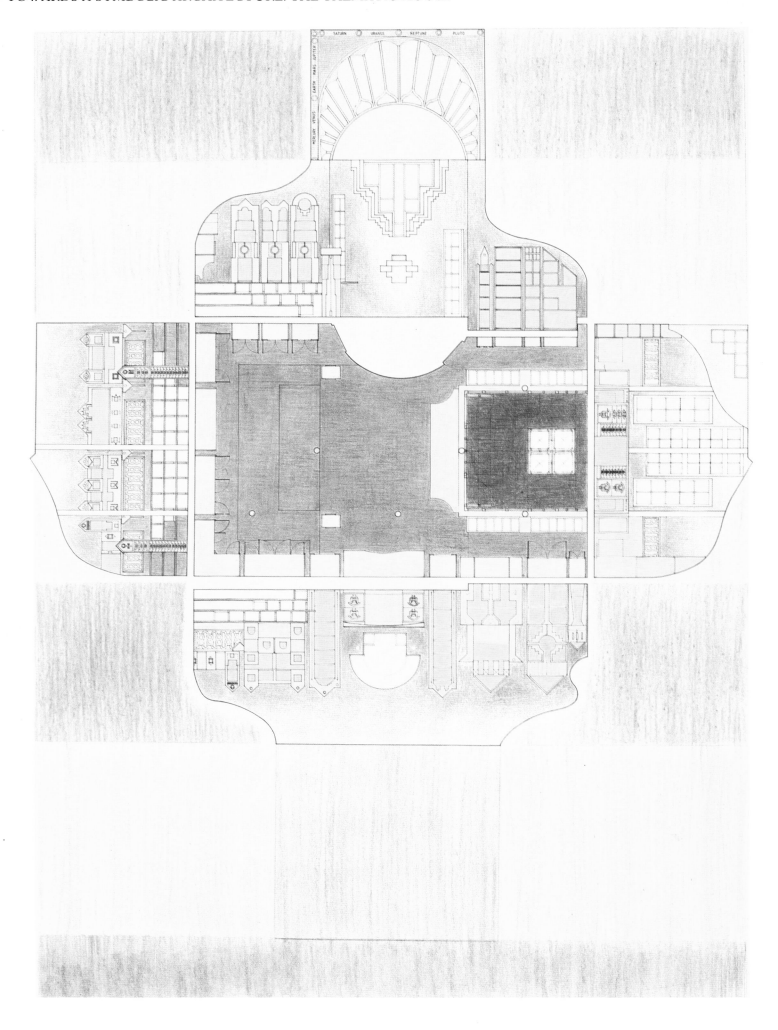

THE BOOKHOUSES

The overall mode of the bookhouses is the same as for the rest of the house: a Free-Style Classicism based on wood construction. The wood allows a flat, planar style which is decorated with black lines or motifs (2).

Thus instead of the usual homogeneity of bookcases – all in the same horizontal International Style of 'dumb boxes', as Robert Venturi has characterised it – there is a variety based on a common material and grammar akin to a successful piece of urbanism – Amsterdam, say, would make a perfect library. Whether the expression of individual periods goes too far is a moot point. I wanted to push the formal expression to a maximum within a restricted colour and material. Thus even the readymade steel filing cabinets are painted to look like Biedermeier wood graining. Two steel skyscrapers – one marked 'T' and the other 'M' – hold traditional and modern architectural slides. These are also made from cheap, readymade storage cabinets, which, since they come in different sizes, can be stacked on top of each other to give a pleasing articulation. The light-tables for viewing slides act also as windows overlooking the dining room and are wood-grained like the rest of the furniture. Only the three chairs are real Biedermeier.

The plan shows the main axis of the room, which focuses on the terrace with its four pyramids (1). The minor axis – marked by face windows at each end – connects the SOLAR STAIR and the view to the west over neighbouring gardens. Reading clockwise from the bottom right, the Egyptian/Doric bookhouse is followed by Early-Roman, Late-Roman, Early-Medieval, Late-Medieval and Early-Renaissance. High-Renaissance is at the corner. The Mannerist, Baroque and Nineteenth-Century bookhouses stand above low windows and the three Post-Modern skyscrapers occupy the top left corner. Banished to the far right corner are the 1930s Moderne, 1950s International Style, Anonymous 1960s and Late-Modern bookscrapers. On the ceiling above are a sunburst, clouds and the nine planets.

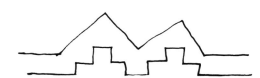

WESTERN ARCHITECTURE

Themes from the history of Western architecture are abstracted and stylised with minimal signs to give slight variations of meaning. The early sketches show the development from Egyptian Doric to Roman to Early- and Late-Medieval. Early-Renaissance is indicated by diagonal shifts – comparable to the North German practice

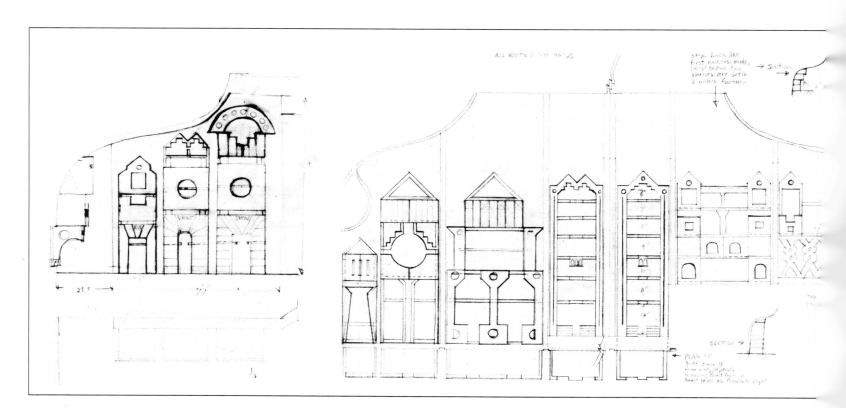

which the High-Renaissance disliked (1). Mannerism is indicated by M-pediments which are broken and inverted (2); Baroque and Rococo by a dance of decorative lines and dots (3); the Nineteenth-Century by a solid geometry, and Post-Modern by anthropomorphism, a current preoccupation (4). The Late-Modern bookscrapers are banished to the corner (5).

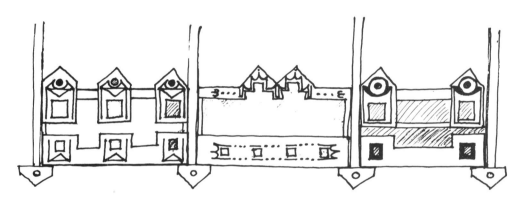

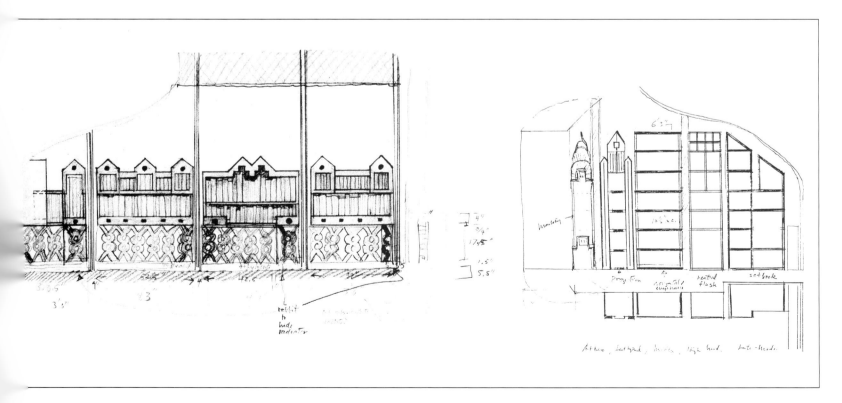

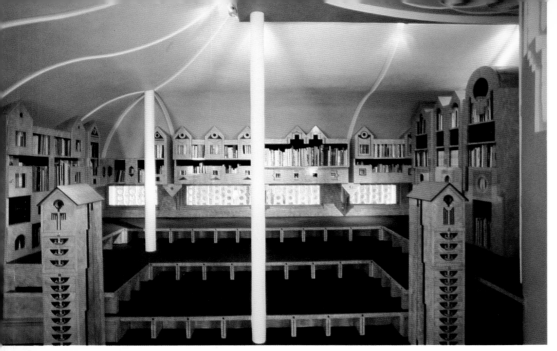

THE LIBRARY AS A VILLAGE

Two areas of seating look towards the greenery outside. The bigger area looks out onto a terrace shaded by an overhanging branch from the large locust tree in a neighbour's garden (4). Maggie insisted we indent the roof in order to keep this branch, hence the strange inner bulge just above the Egyptian bookhouse (2). There are steps opposite this seating area which rise on three sides to form a group of terraces, carpeted thickly as if they were green banks to sit on. Eight or ten people can recline on these terraces and watch slides or a film on the screen which can be raised and fixed to a pole behind the desk (1).

While the comprehensive views of the library show a variety of shapes – the result of several symbolic programmes – the details have more harmony since each bookhouse, or element, is complete in itself. If there is a dissonance at times, it is akin to that of the village High Street, where different buildings compete for attention within a shared style. Whether a library should try to replicate an urban landscape is of course arguable, but I prefer that idea to the usual urban cemetery of bookshelves.

Antonello da Messina, *S. Jerome in his Study*. S. Jerome's study became a model for scholars copied in the Renaissance idea of the *studiolo* – a hidden retreat full of secret drawers, *trompe l'oeil* and trick latches behind which were kept books and treasures. Antonello da Messina followed previous painters in making S. Jerome and his *studiolo* appear as a particularly appealing mixture of monumentality, domesticity and openness, a combination we have tried to emulate. (Reproduced by courtesy of the Trustees, The National Gallery, London)

THE SOLAR STAIR FACE

I designed the S-curve of the roof to suggest the swell of a canvas tent, while Terry Farrell worked out its overall structure which resulted in nine supporting ribs (2). Since the SOLAR STAIR and SUNWELL are the focus for this ceiling, the nine planets became an obvious subject for symbolic expression, and each of the nine light fixtures is assigned the name of a planet according to its distance from the SUNWELL.

The original symbolic programme reads:

Above the head, through the sun wall, burst the sunrays – illuminating darkness and stupidity. The enlightenment of ideas breaks through the truth – peels it back layer after layer – showing surface, then insulation, then structure, so the decoration is the Truth revealed, both on the sun wall and in the dark sky. Its clouds are shown as black billows like the approaching night, while on the other side, the light of the nine planets casts through evil a sharp beam that falls on the books.

Thus Thought and Imagination together crack open Truth to reveal Her hidden beauty. After which She is collected into the series of architectural books.

The stair contains many layers of symbolism. A face motif, one of thirty variations in the house, is peeled back to reveal the construction of the cylinder. This structure, designed by David French and Terry Farrell, is an ingenious *tour de force* which holds up the adjacent chimneys as well as the stair itself – which also adds to its strength. To demonstrate the way the cylinder has been constructed, a 'peeling face' window reveals the layers – stucco, brick, reinforced concrete, brick, stucco – in line with the Modernist doctrine of 'truth to materials' (1). Here, these materials are painted to harmonise with colours of the room, rather than remain simply straightforward (3).

This window also reveals the swing of the curving stair rails behind and leads the eye up to its crown, or hair, overhead. This is another sunburst, as in the chimneys outside or the London columns within. Inevitably it is bursting through London clouds which are also peeled back in billows of purple-blue to show they are heavy with rain. The colour of storm clouds was imitated in the stippling.

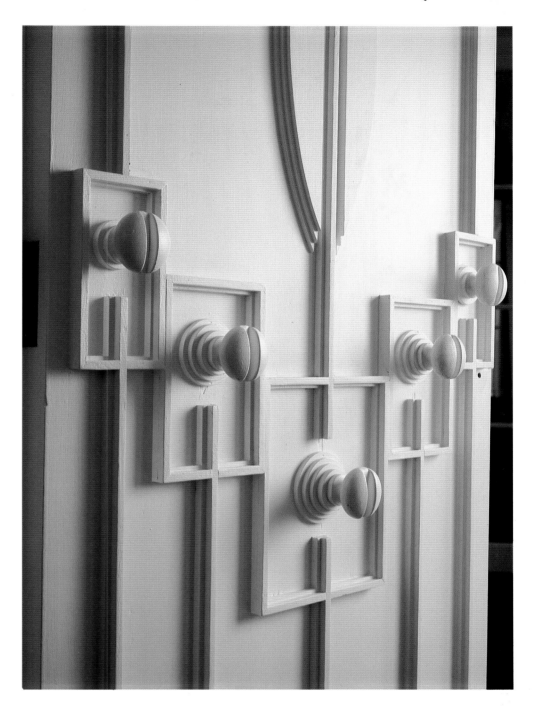

12: THE FOURSQUARE ROOM

The square and rectangle have been the prevalent forms in ninety per cent of all architecture since the grid-based cities of the Egyptians and Chinese. Despite eulogies to the circle and triangle by die-hards such as Buckminster Fuller, the square world has continued to be architecture's physical and metaphysical constant. The FOURSQUARE ROOM celebrates this idea.

The door, which ironically has five rather than four handles, opens into a white and cream room with windows on all sides. The square window, with four equal quadrants, is the basis of the ornamental motif used on the ceiling and floor to orientate the room to the four cardinal points and to the four civilisations that most affect us personally – Egypt, China, Europe and America. Almost everything, including the epigrams, rugs and furniture, expresses this obsessive theme. But inevitably a counter-theme has crept in – for instance in the fireplace the ABA motif, the triplet, is more interesting for being different.

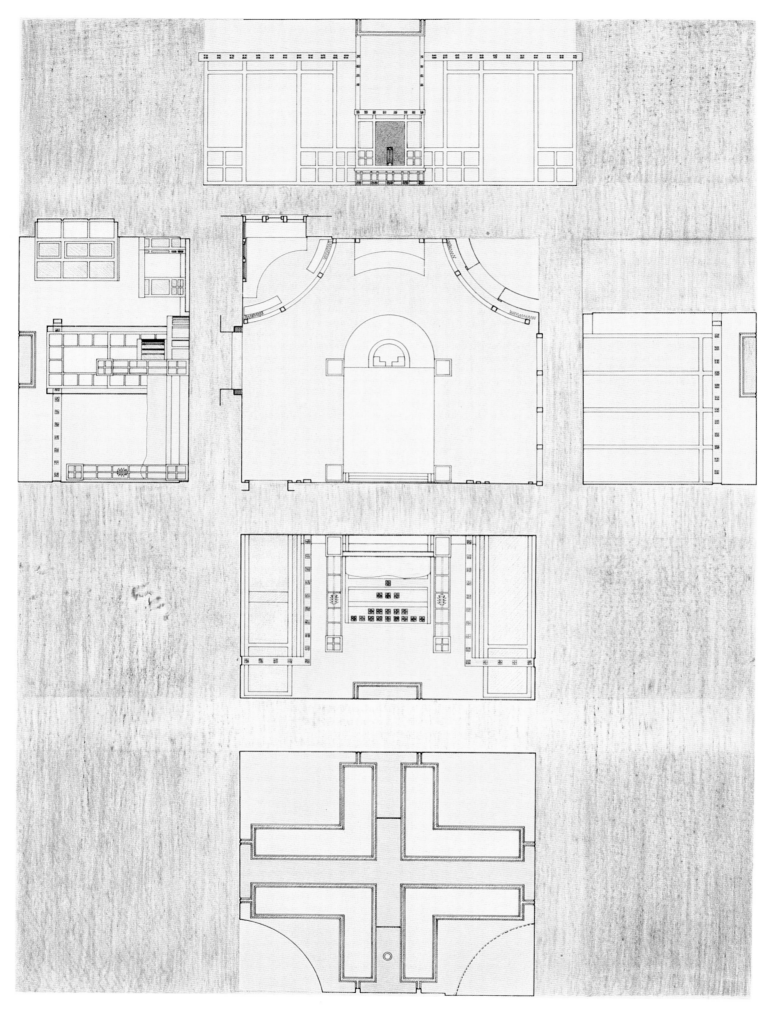

FOURNESS

The foursquare theme did not occur to us until we had explored and rejected many other, more complicated ideas. It is based on the repetitive use of the most simple constructional element, the four-by-four inch wooden pier. Since I wanted this to become an ordering, as well as structural, device it is used on all four sides of the room, either as a colonnade or a screen. Subdivided, it is used in flat bands to hold mirrors on the ceiling or lights and books around the bed. At first I thought of this structural element as the most primitive unornamented Tuscan order. Then when I used it on the curves of the stair and fireplace walls I realised that the Palladian ABA motif could also be modified and used. It wasn't until the decorative purple quadrants were added, to form a band that runs along both horizontal and vertical surfaces, that I thought of Mackintosh's work, although people perceive his influence immediately.

The foursquare organisation of the room inevitably imposes a frontality on the viewer (all the photographs here express this). Thus one unconsciously projects a conceptual grid, and Cartesian x,y,z coordinates, onto the space and objects, and becomes more conscious of the difference in proportion between one square or rectangle and the next. When one gets on axis, the whole room becomes a one-point perspective of harmonic relations.

The cross-axes of the ceiling mirrors create a nervous effect overhead, although after lying in bed for a while I find they become more a focus of interest than tiring. Basically the cross-axes anchor the four-poster bed, and together they dominate the room. Four lights at the top of each corner post again define the cross-axes, while the curved seat and mirrored back centre forcefully (and phallically) on the fireplace. When a pressure catch is touched, a television set emerges out of the curve of the seat. Bedside reading lights are adapted from standard garden lamps which, with their tiers of roofs, resemble pagodas. The four posts of the bed also contain wastebaskets, books, a hi-fi and other functional elements, so what looks like a bizarre, white fantasy is actually quite useful.

The drawings here show some of the explorations made to unravel the formal properties of fourness and tie them into cultural or semantic aspects of the tetramorph – the four corners of the earth, the four times of the day, etc (2). The way the room partially opens into the MOONWELL and BATHPOOL can be seen in plan (1,3). Some people find this openness disorienting, but after a while, when one understands the space and sees how the elements reflect the light and provide unexpected views, their logic becomes clear. Basically they make the room a changing light-catcher.

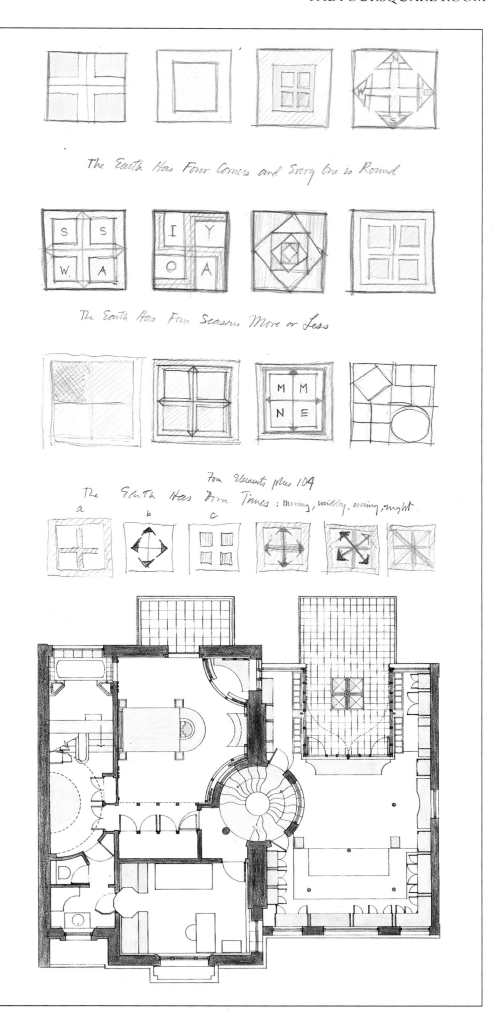

EPIGRAMS

To give the concept of fourness another dimension, and twist, we have stencilled epigrams which either emphasise the theme or deflect it. Thus the bed frame has the traditional saying: *'FOUR CORNERS HAS MY BED / FOUR ANGELS AT MY HEAD / MARK, MATTHEW, LUKE AND JOHN / BLESS THE BED THAT I LIE ON'* (3). The cornice above it has a slight variation on convention: *'THE EARTH HAS FOUR SEASONS, MORE OR LESS'* – the exceptions most familiar to us being the three seasons of Los Angeles and the five of New England. Below this is another epigram: *'THE EARTH HAS FOUR CORNERS, ALL ROUND'* – again a traditional saying varied for this specific context, where the surfaces are curved, almost round. (In any case, the earth has no corners and *is* round). Across from this, behind the raised TV (1) on the fireplace architrave, is: *'THE EARTH HAS FOUR ELEMENTS, ONE HUNDRED AND FOUR'.* This underlines the difference between our view of the universe and the Greeks'. In the future we shall add two literary conceits – Rudyard Kipling's: *'FOUR THINGS GREATER THAN ALL THINGS ARE / WOMEN AND HORSES AND POWER AND WAR',* and Dorothy Parker's answer: *'FOUR BE THE THINGS I'D BETTER BE WITHOUT / LOVE, CURIOSITY, FRECKLES AND DOUBT'.*

Apparently the Chinese emperors identified with the annual course of the sun and 'embraced' the four points of the compass, even living each season in a different quadrant of their square palaces. In researching the concept of fourness and the tetramorph I came up with the following traditional equations: east symbolises Spring, air, infancy, dawn, the crescent moon and a sanguinary temperament; south is a sign of Summer, fire, youth, midday, the full moon and a nervous disposition; west is Autumn, water, middle age, evening, the waning moon and a lymphatic personality; north is Winter, earth, old age, night, the new moon and a bilious mood. This symbolic system is followed in part on the ground floor using colours and themes and will someday be recapitulated here in the four corners of the four-poster. Thomas Tresham's Triangular Lodge (see Chapter I, Part II) was always in my mind as an example of a numerical and symbolic idea pursued with consistency.

THE WINDOW SEAT WINDOW

A window obviously frames a view of the world outside as well as whatever is placed in front of it. It also lets in light and the glass surface either reflects this light or itself becomes slightly luminous. Lastly, the window is a metaphor for our eyes. Our windows on the world are the viewpoints which we either choose or inherit and although imaginative fiction or other people's stories may provide further perspectives, we can never escape having a viewpoint, or several. For this reason we have made windows on the world a major theme of the house – and of the curious chair illustrated here.

The back of the chair resembles two sash windows. It has three differently proportioned panes to allow for its flared seat, and has the words *WINDOW SEAT WINDOW* stencilled on the horizontal surface of its back (3). Perhaps its most remarkable aspect is the way it can function as a movable part of the room, as if it were a detachable piece of wall (4). It thus becomes a double pun: a window seat next to a window that is a seat made from windows.

Vermeer and De Hooch often painted interiors in which a window is seen spilling light obliquely onto a domestic scene (2). In Vermeer's *Lady at the Virginals with a Gentleman,* the notion that music restores bodily health as well as soothes the spirit is implicitly equated with the soft light that comes through the side windows; the notion is spelled out in the epigram on the virginal: 'music is the companion of joy, the medicine of sadness'. The mirror reflecting the lady is in a sense equated with a window revealing her face. Thus the windows, mirror and geometrically disposed room give this painting an air of domestic peace.

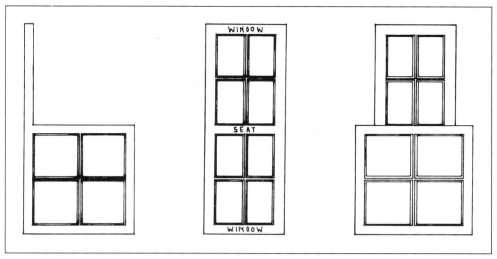

Johannes Vermeer (1632-1675) *Lady at the Virginals with a Gentleman* (Reproduced by Gracious Permission of Her Majesty The Queen)

THE BATHPOOL

Opening off the bedroom from two points is the main bathroom, which resembles a greenish pool. Much of this room was designed by Maggie, who insisted that the bath have a view of the garden (4) and that the space be connected, acoustically, to the bedroom (1). Interesting perspective effects are created by the lights and mirrors placed symmetrically on either side of the stepped frame in front of the bath – which to us resembles the entrance to a grotto (2). The water line is indicated by tiles which continue to the higher level of the bedroom floor (3). Thus from the landing one has the illusion of descending into a body of blue-green water with lots of ripples and eddies – an effect created by the mottled tiles baked in various shades of sub-aqueous colour. These are arranged in graduated sets to give intense areas of coloured activity, rather like the ocean surface on a stormy day. The top set of tiles has a continuous frieze of breakers rolling towards the shore – the landing. These are designed as alternating face motifs and establish a rhythm of 'two ducks to the bar'. Jay Bonner worked with us and made the tiles himself.

JACOB'S LADDER

At Terry Farrell's suggestion, we kept the original stairs in this part of the house to connect the half-levels of the BATHPOOL and dressing room above it (3). This proved to be a very useful way of squeezing in more space as well as providing a reminder of what the house was like before its conversion. I used the stair motif as a repetitive decorative device at several scales to create the idea of many steps (2). The vertical units are for storing socks and ties, while at the top, the figure of the man-in-the-mirror (Jacob) holds suits. Jacob's dream, while lying on a rock, of angels climbing a ladder to heaven, has formed the excuse for displaying some Chinese rocks and roots which I very much admire (1). For the Chinese these rocks symbolised the heavenly land of the immortals, so their connection with Jacob's dream is not without reason.

13: THE TOP FLOOR LANDING

The top floor landing provides a respite from all the previous and subsequent imagery. Cool and abstract, coloured in turquoise, cream and white, it is designed as a transitional space without any assertive themes of its own. At the end opposite the SOLAR STAIR, the MOONWELL provides a suggestion of crescent shapes and flares with half-moon sconce lights. The doors are treated with varying abstract patterns, although they are more richly decorated on the other side. The double doorknobs, which are grooved in the centre, can be seen as the buds of growing plants and the split ovals as a feminine sign.

After designing doors for several years I have come to one modest conclusion which I pass on to the world: the single doorknob is an oversight of nature. The door, like the human body that passes through it, was meant to be symmetrical. It is quite true that doors usually open from one side and are hinged on the other, but this functional necessity should not distract us from the greater visual and conceptual truth. The typical Classical door has decorative panels set symmetrically within the symmetrical frame around it. The overhead pediment and surrounding ornament are also symmetrically disposed in order to centre our focus of approach. The body, with its two arms and two legs, approaches the door frontally – Q.E.D., the single doorknob is a mistake, a mere utilitarian afterthought, longing to be completed by its better half, its partner. The world has yet to thank me for this discovery, although I suppose doorknob manufacturers soon will.

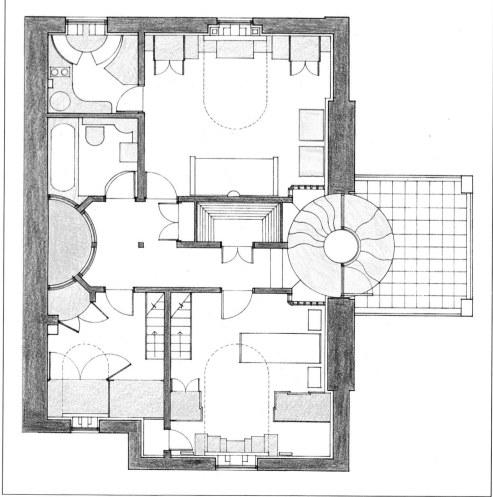

DOORS

The decoration of the doors opening off the landing is in each case organised symmetrically (1,2). Johnny's Room is identified with back-to-back Js; Lily's Room by two Ls. On the floor below, Maggie's study is signified by the abstract representation of an M above an opened book (3). The book is also organised in a chevron pattern and relates to the vertical lines of the rest of the decoration. The representational and compositional requirements are thus given equal weight.

The doors in every case are readymade, hollow-core constructions to which stepped mouldings and double doorknobs have been added. The cheap wooden knob allows cutting and painting to form part of the overall system, thus showing once again that an integrated, meaningful architecture need not be expensive. Applied ornament is here midway between aesthetic logic and symbolism.

Photo: Ianthe Ruthven

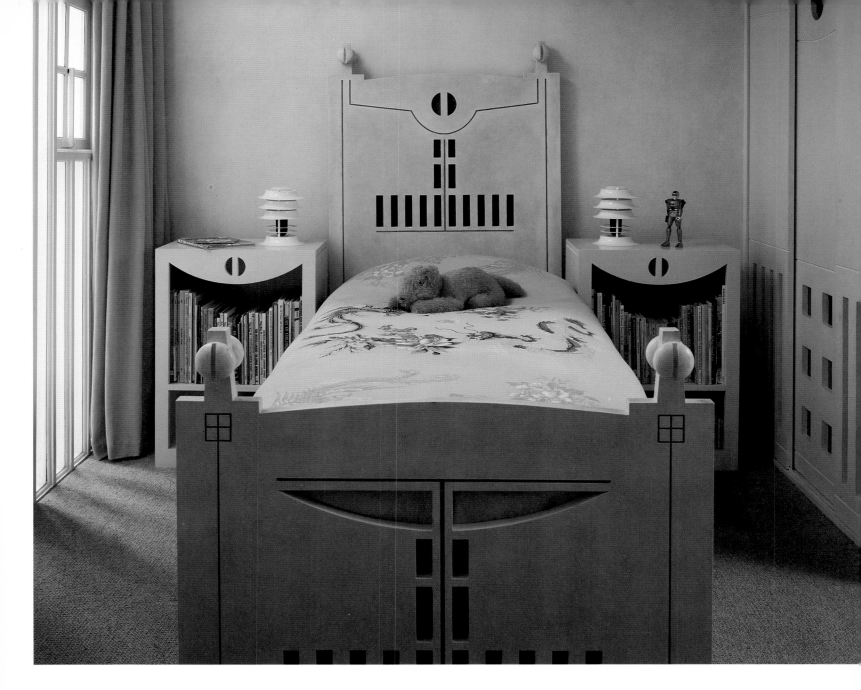

14: JOHNNY'S ROOM

The first room on the top floor belongs to our son Johnny, and since his favourite colour is blue, we used this colour combined with a complementary cream. His initials are transformed in various ways on the door and bed, the Js stylised with other patterns so that suggestive veiling, ambiguity and double meaning all combine to make the emblem less explicit. For instance a horizontal is added at the base of the letter at the foot of the bed to form a face motif. The J on the headboard has cut-out globes with solid centres – a form repeated on the bedside tables and then turned inside out, as it were, on the bed pinnacles. These are, in fact, the same double doorknobs as on the door, now used as decorative accents or crowns. The phrase 'with knobs on' means 'something extra special' – and so we consider our son.

Although the main dormer window to the right faces north, warm south and west light spills in from the SOLAR STAIR and the sleeping balcony above. As in much attic space, the curves, left-over corners and contradictions between wall and roof planes make for pleasing surprises and sculptural variety. This has been emphasised by painting the shapes slightly different shades of blue.

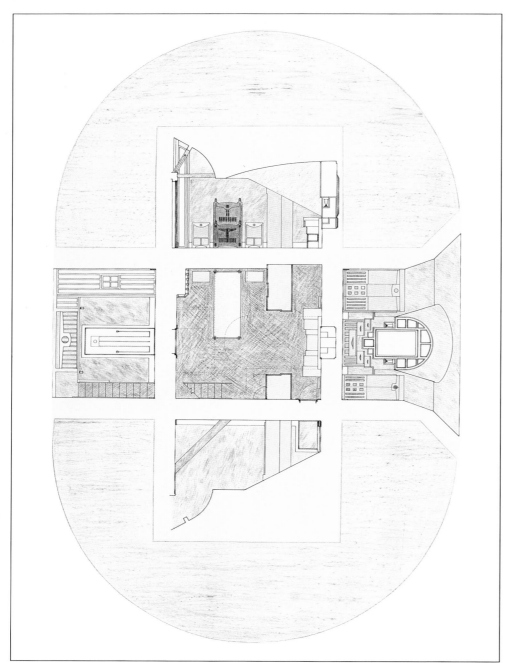

FACES AND PLANTS

The existing attic rooms were pokey, low and badly lit, so we decided to open them out to create more space, light and view. The view was gained by cutting dormer windows into the pitched roof; these leave a sculpted shape – a barrel-vault in forced perspective – on axis with the door. On entering the room in daytime one is immediately drawn towards the view of the trees framed by a blue canopy (4). The window shade has a stylised St John's Wort, screen-printed by Valentine Abbott, placed above the stagger motif (3). Again the idea was to abstract a set of patterns so they would fit the context yet still be recognisable.

Initially I thought of the room as divided vertically into three levels like an Egyptian temple: a base of cross-hatched earth, a lower section of growing reeds and a top of flared petals, sun and blue sky (2). When the room was actually built these divisions were simplified into a lower level of rectangular voids and an upper level of circles and sky. This theme is developed in the details of the extra sleeping loft which Terry Farrell squeezed in above the bedroom. The motifs used in this space reserved for youth (it's too low for adults) are those found throughout the house – the oval, face and windows on the world, all executed in a flat planar style.

15: LILY'S ROOM

Lily's Room is one of the smallest in the house since she, two-years-old at the time of design, was the smallest member of the family. She now sleeps on her future desk, which has a pivotal side to keep her from falling out. When she is older she will move upstairs to the sleeping loft which is connected to her room.

There are many stylisations of lilies in the room which Maggie and I worked out, including one giant group that pulls up as a window shade. This blocks out the light from the face window and hides the flat surfaces which attract a lot of animals and toys. Although tiny, the room seems bigger because of a large mirror on one side, the curved space that opens onto the MOONWELL and sleeping loft above, and the colours (variants of the washed creams and turquoise used on the landing) – so that when the door is open the space outside appears to be part of the room.

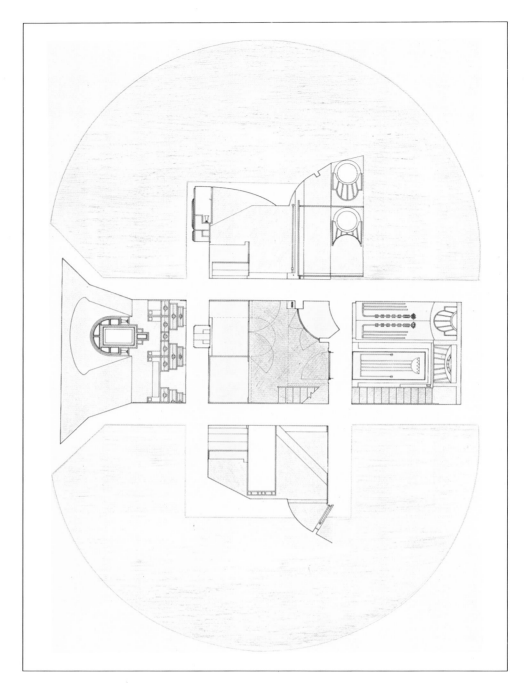

THE STYLISATION OF LILIES

When representing a particular object or idea I usually begin by making ten or twelve transformations of the form, starting from literal versions – photographs and paintings – and then moving in different directions towards an abstract representation. Some of these steps can be seen here. The first sketches (3) are like turn-of-the-century lilies, and are influenced by Art Nouveau designers and artists such as William Morris. Most of them are obviously somewhat stylised, as if for a wallpaper design; in the sketch of the female tiger springing out of a tiger lily, the swirls of the flower form an aesthetic system. We explored the potential of my two favourite lilies, lily of the valley and the lilies depicted on the Cretan frescoes of Amnisos, but in the end we narrowed the field down to something more geometric: a version of the water lily (5,6). This motif was used on the wardrobe and door (7). Set at the top of stems that shoot up over voids, the flowers are depicted as reaching for the sunrays that provide a counter-form. These rays were to have stylised hands, similar to those introduced during the monotheistic sun cult of Akhenaten. Thus lilies and sunrays were to reach towards each other and shake hands (4).

We have used the same family of forms in this room as in the rest of the house, but varied it slightly. For example, the desk/bed has sliding drawers which form a face motif when doubled by the reflection in the mirror. Maggie, who designed the stylised lily and the desk/bed, used a descending curve above an interlocked stagger, an inversion of the window face behind (2). From her desk Lily can look over her wardrobe into the MOONWELL and at certain moments see the moon reflected in the mirror engraved with its image.

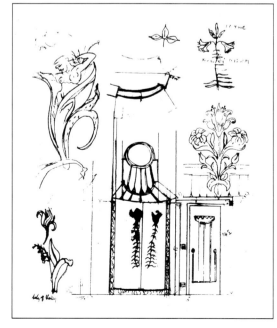

16: NAN'S ROOM

Ann Laycock, who looks after Johnny and Lily, has one of the nicest rooms in the house, with a view south over the garden high above the trees. Nan, as she is known to many of her friends and charges, likes cats and so several of the images here are based on stylised faces both of cats and of those birds which resemble them – owls. The bed is a 'two-poster' with curtains on either side. On the back of the door is a stylised logo – Nan. Since one of her favourite colours is yellow, this is used with a complementary light grey and white. The COSMIC OVAL has as part of its sentence '*PERSONAL SIGNS / OWLS, LILIES, CATS / FIX A PLACE IN TIME*' — a reference to this top floor. The floor as a whole is unified by a grey-blue carpet which runs throughout.

The window shade has a stylised image of the garden below, so the concept can be compared with reality. When it is down, daylight floods into the curved dormer and reflects off the yellow surfaces to give the room a cheerful glow even on grey days.

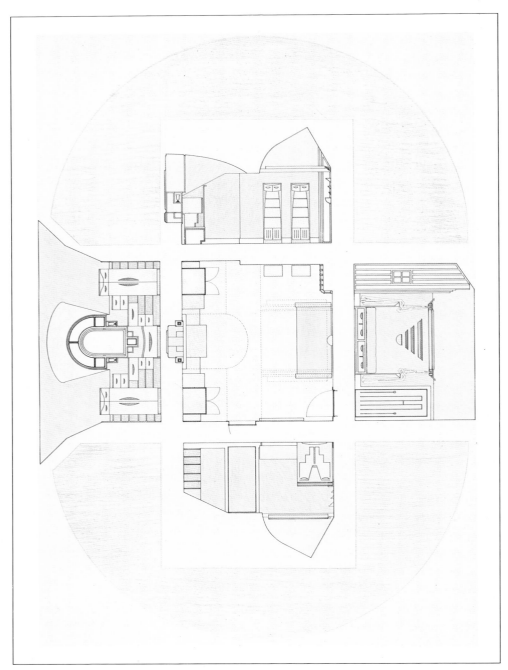

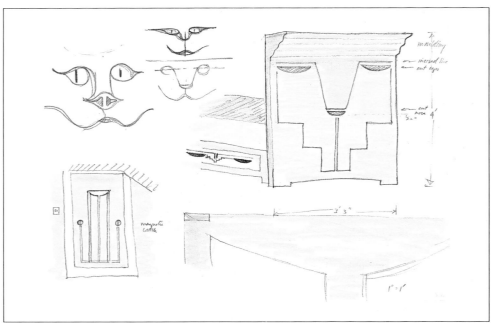

OWLS AND CATS

The storage wall, with the window at its centre, is made up of staggered drawers which step up and out to the wardrobes (owls) in the corners. The seat/drawer, with its smile, contains more storage space. Flat surfaces are usually filled with pictures since one of Nan's hobbies is photography. On the headboards of the bed and the bed drawers are abstractions of a cat's face, and on the door leading into the kitchen is a cat's bowl.

17: THE DOME OF WATER

The DOME OF WATER is based loosely on Borromini's S. Carlo alle Quattro Fontane. Initially, we had asked Piers Gough to design a jacuzzi, for which he thought of using upside-down Jencksianas for the elevations. The idea of using green tiles *overhead* to represent the earth developed naturally from this inversion (and was also Piers' idea). Since the available space was rectangular and we wanted a curved, communal space in which six people could sit, an oval was the inevitable choice. As I had been lecturing on Baroque illusionist domes, I suggested Borromini's Quattro Fontane as a reference. Simon Sturgis produced a version of the triangular layout designs Borromini had used, Piers Gough designed the illusionistic coffers in terrazzo and brass, and Ilinca Cantacuzino and I designed the light-pendentives based on the four seasons. The greens of the terrazzo and tiles relate to the adjacent garden and garden rooms. While we were pondering the notion I found a partial precedent in a Roman villa being excavated in Britain which had a circular pool with a ritualistic function centred in a grid plan.

THE STYLISATION OF THEMES

The themes or concepts we decide on in the course of the design process are continually transformed to make them relate more closely to the physical context, to the other themes and to their own internal composition. Thus the process is continuous and circular, or perhaps spiral, with its connotations of zeroing-in, of aiming towards a synthesis. For the themes of the four seasons and of the twelve months – or zodiac – used on the jacuzzi, Ilinca Cantacuzino and I did some research on conventional motifs.

For example for Spring we etched and painted new versions of March, April and May at the top of the circular light. These were counter-balanced by roses at the bottom so that one's eye travels in a circle, pausing at the five accentuated points. The rose is a symbol of Spring love; the sword and hawthorn in the centre are also signs of the season. My painting on the glass is an attempt to integrate these disparate forms with tonal areas of light green, yellow and amber. Ilinca Cantacuzino oversaw the production of these designs.

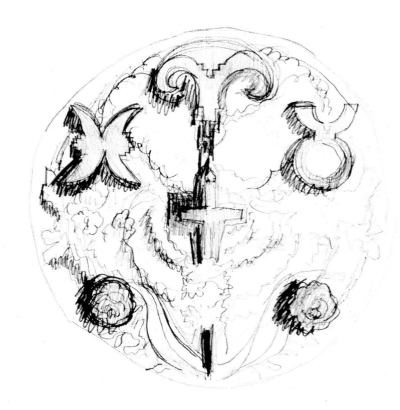

18: THE TIME GARDEN

The TIME GARDEN is not yet finished. However, the south-facing rectangle has been divided into four quadrants which have been shifted west ten feet to centre on the house and its double stairway. The two long sides are bounded by walls of trellis and half-mirrored doors – windows on the world – that divide the walk around the garden into twelve parts representing the twelve months of the year. In the future wall plaques or sculpture will define these areas as at Edzell Castle, one of the places which inspired us.

Maggie has designed the overall layout, topiary and planting as a route running clockwise around the site. Starting from the east, or Spring side, one moves south up a brick path under an old pear tree, then west and finally north, under an umbrella-shaped American chestnut. The path changes pattern and slope with each direction to introduce variety into the rectilinear plan. In the future the four cardinal points will be given further symbolic elaboration according to a programme, although the basic structure is already clear. For instance one can see the way the double stair jumps across a cross-axis and over the paved windows on the world. Thus the hard play area where the children can bicycle is separated from the soft planted area for picnics. Curved motifs are contrasted with staggers, as in the rest of the house.

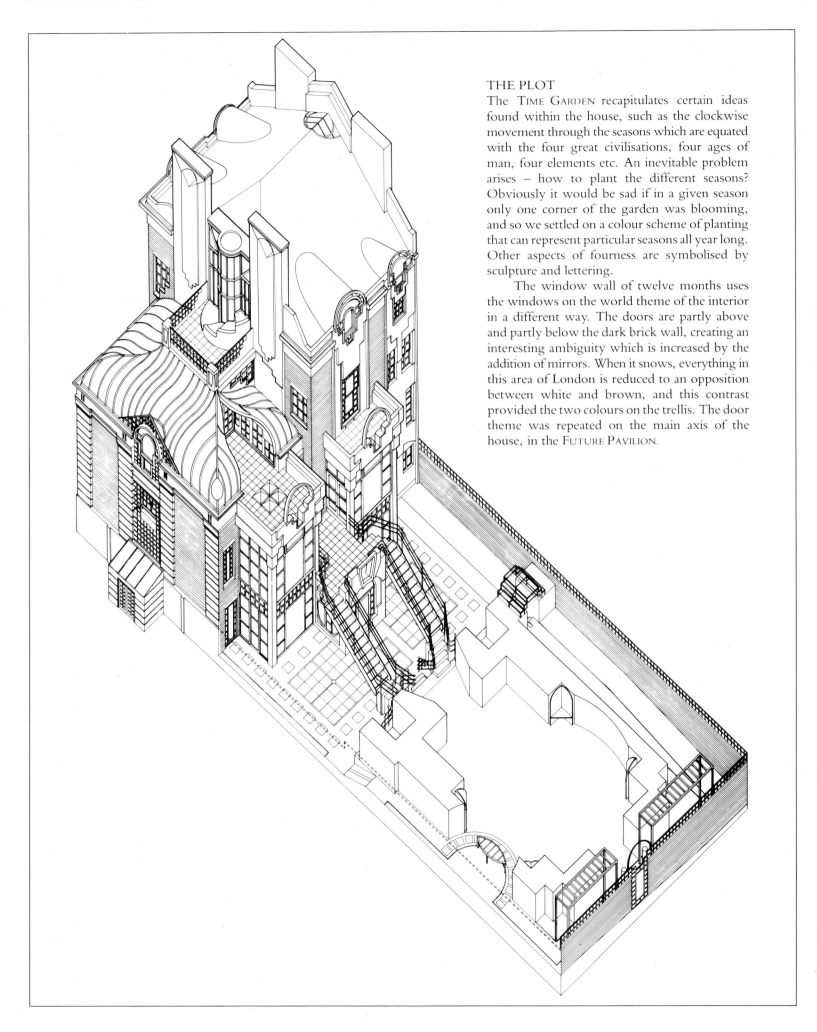

THE PLOT

The TIME GARDEN recapitulates certain ideas found within the house, such as the clockwise movement through the seasons which are equated with the four great civilisations, four ages of man, four elements etc. An inevitable problem arises – how to plant the different seasons? Obviously it would be sad if in a given season only one corner of the garden was blooming, and so we settled on a colour scheme of planting that can represent particular seasons all year long. Other aspects of fourness are symbolised by sculpture and lettering.

The window wall of twelve months uses the windows on the world theme of the interior in a different way. The doors are partly above and partly below the dark brick wall, creating an interesting ambiguity which is increased by the addition of mirrors. When it snows, everything in this area of London is reduced to an opposition between white and brown, and this contrast provided the two colours on the trellis. The door theme was repeated on the main axis of the house, in the FUTURE PAVILION.

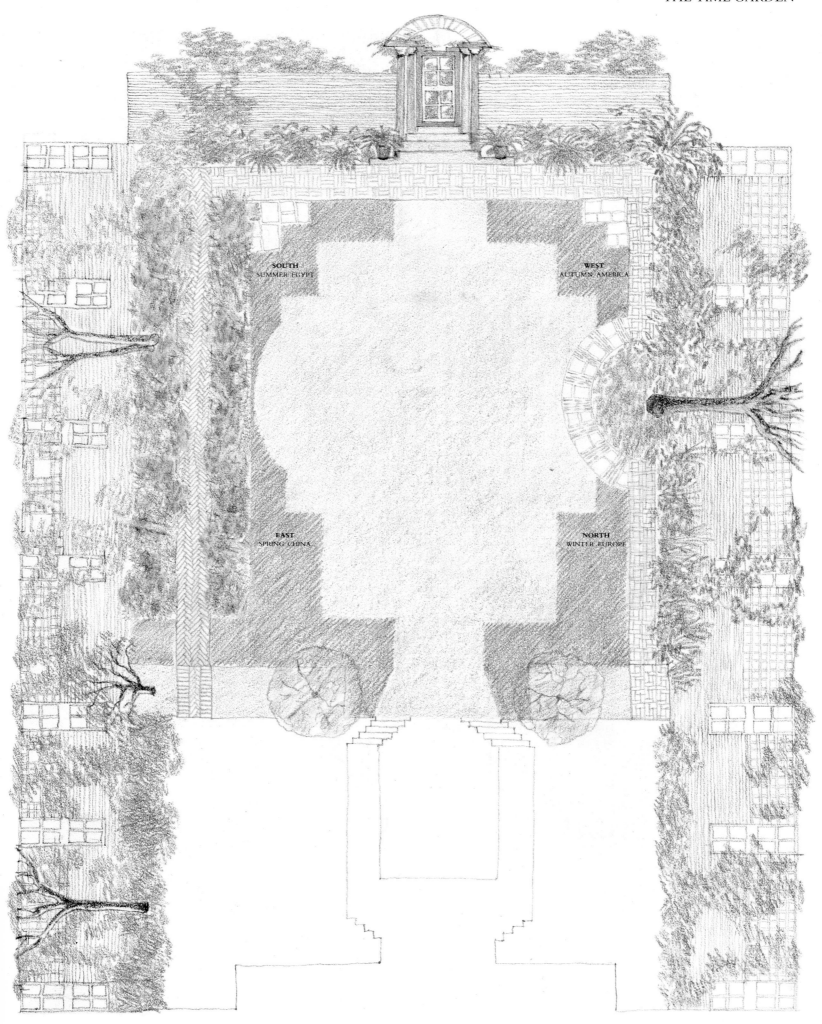

THE FUTURE PAVILION

The FUTURE PAVILION is an eyecatcher at the end of the garden on axis with the centre of the house. It has a forced perspective that focuses on a mirrored door/window that looks as if it opens into the next garden. The notion of *trompe l'oeil,* which we have used throughout the house, was intended here as an allusion to seeing into the future, over the garden wall as it were.

The future as shaped and distorted by the past is a constant theme of Classical art. One of the standard legends drawn on by realistic painters – that of Zeuxis and the bird that was so deceived by some painted grapes that it tried to peck one off the canvas – has alas found an echo in this *trompe l'oeil.* One day, soon after it was completed, a swallow tried to fly through the mirrored door with disastrous results; if it happens again we shall paint an eagle, or some other predator, on the mirror flying the other way.

As one approaches this pavilion lettering on the door becomes visible: 'THE FUTURE'. Then one looks down to the plinth where it says 'IS BEHIND YOU'. When the eye shifts to the mirror, the reflected view is framed by the backs of the two piers which have two sentences written vertically and in reverse so they can only be read in the mirror: 'E ARRIVA DAL PASSATO TROPPO PRESTO' and 'A LA RECHERCHE DU TEMPS QUI VIENT'.

CHAPTER VI
The Style of Meaning

THERE IS MORE TO SYMBOLIC ARCHITECTURE THAN its message. Paradoxically, symbolism brings out aesthetics – its opposite – because it gives the designer an ordered mandate for expressive form. In this century he has lacked these directives with the result that questions of style have become suppressed. Either the architect has claimed that the style he adopted was a consequence of economy and technology, or else he has presented it as pure art, a result of his formal mastery. Either way style and expression have suffered because they have become private, ultimately a matter of personal taste. By constrast, a symbolic programme worked out between architect and client establishes a public meaning that can be debated. It allows for disagreements and in turn calls for commitment from both parties. And this public commitment can allow the architect to design with greater aesthetic force because he knows which values to express and which to suppress. This is especially true if, as I am suggesting, the symbolic programme is actually part of the building contract and invented equally by architect and client. Then the content of expressive form is explicit, and the more motivated the content, the more charged will be the form. Meaning liberates form; a symbolic programme sanctions expression.

There is a certain resistance to symbolic architecture. When taking people through the Thematic House, I notice that whether they like the building or not, many regard my explanations as either reductive or superfluous. Perhaps as a result of having been constantly reminded this century that 'a poem should not mean, but be' people think that, by the same token, architecture is supposed to present its own peculiar truths and not deliver up a meaning. An awareness of the literal meaning of a form, its motive and conceit, reduces the experience of the architectural totality to just one of its facets. Susan Sontag puts this point forcefully in her treatise *Against Interpretation* when she argues against an hermeneutics and in favour of an 'erotics of art'. As soon as we explain anything, we reduce perception to a frame of reference.

There are others who regard the symbolism of the Thematic House as completely redundant, an irrelevant appendage to the architecture. They admit it may have been a motive for the designer, but believe it is of no importance to the perceiver. These people are not necessarily committed to Modernist doctrines, or to pure aesthetic experience; their modes of perception probably reflect the mental attitudes of our time and are likely to be widely shared. These attitudes are not so much wrong, I would argue, as specific to our period. Just as in the Gothic period one might have been able to *read* a cathedral quite spontaneously, in our time we *experience* a museum, or the paintings within it; we don't try to read explanations, or search for the artist's intentions, or ask what a building or object signifies.

This reluctance to know and understand may be partly a matter of taste, or of timing. One may prefer to have additional knowledge supplied either before or after an aesthetic experience, although one of the pleasures of experiencing symbolic design is to learn and perceive simultaneously – to discover intended, and dissonant, meanings, *as one sees*. In this sense, knowledge, writing, stencilled labels, metaphorical images, hints and cues are neither reductive nor superfluous but an essential ingredient of *style*. Without them the excitement of the pursuit is lost – as it would be in a detective story with no plot.

But this leads to another objection: 'Sherlock Holmes is all very well for children, but like narrative painting, it is a low genre of art'. This line of reasoning has an impressive pedigree. It is confined not only to Modernists, since many Classicists stress the merits of idealism over realism, abstraction over representation. Narrative art, like narrative fiction, tends to be regarded as inferior because it sacrifices the universal to the particular, a breadth of vision to a quick, but narrow, understanding. The higher faculties of the mind, it has been argued since Plato, are usurped by the lower ones: it is easier to understand a parable than a mathematical truth, a cloying appeal to the senses than a geometrical concept, ornament than abstract space.

Although these arguments contain some truth, the conclusions which have often been drawn from them in both art and architecture are false: namely that ornament and narrative should not exist, or should be relegated to a secondary role. While blatant meanings may momentarily cloud the intellect they can also – as Abbot Suger argued in the twelfth century when defending the use of Gothic ornament and stained glass – lead the mind to higher levels of organisation. Indeed in poetry, sensual apprehension is traditionally simultaneous with thought. As T. S. Eliot wrote of the metaphysical poets: '[They] could feel their thought as immediately as the odour of a rose'.

For a long time, the work of Baroque and Rococo architects such as Borromini and Neumann was considered a lower form of art because it gave importance to ornament, figural sculpture and imagery. And even recent writers such as Siegfried Giedion and Christian Otto have discussed the architecture of these periods in terms of space, structure and light rather than as an iconographic totality.

Mental habits die hard and it takes time for new ones to be born. But if we did learn an appreciation of the symbolic a whole range of new pleasures would open up to us, one of which would be the dramatic search for meaning. This is not a simple game with a single solution, but rather a complex drama with several subplots and possible endings. And the purpose of the drama is to impel the viewers forward in directions which they, or perhaps even the designer, may not have imagined. One surprising feature of symbolic design is that it creates in the perceiver the expectation of meanings: visitors to the Elemental House are often provoked to discover plausible new meanings even where none are intended. Architecture, like all art, is multi-layered in a way that allows different paths to be found through its web of meanings. Hence one defence of symbolic design is its interest for the beholder: it encourages a dynamic reading and the invention of new interpretations.

1 Philip Pearlstein, *Lantern, S. Ivo,* 1983 (watercolour on paper 30½ x 21½in). In Borromini's S. Ivo della Sapienza, heterogeneous forms and ideas are pulled together *formally* by the spiral and *thematically* by the main subject – *Sapienza*, 'Divine Wisdom'. Wisdom is learned, it is implied, by mounting steps and making spiral leaps which reach upwards to higher and higher levels of abstraction. Pearlstein's watercolour dramatises this spiritual and intellectual ascent by contrasting the domes with the common base of pantiles. (Courtesy the Frumkin Gallery, New York)

HYBRID OR INTEGRATED?

That a symbolic work is perceived differently from an abstract one leads to the next query: is there a specific *style* of meaning? If the same question is asked of realist painting, to which symbolic architecture is related, then according to such writers as Linda Nochlin and Frank Goodyear, the answer is no. There is not just one form of realism in art, but many, and their methods and goals differ. The same is true to some extent of symbolic architecture, which has different modes with a common basis. As Linda Nochlin points out, realist painting is based partly on the device of metonymy – the contiguity of many represented objects. Although Philip Pearlstein's realist watercolour (1) may have a minimum of narrative or symbolic intention, a system of meaning is nonetheless created by the metonymic relationships – the relation of domes to roofs, to globes and to each other. The mottled pantiles form a general base over which these redundant forms bob and we can thus infer a meaning, whether the painter intended it or not: for instance the rising and sinking of monumental forms within the city.

Symbolic architecture builds up meanings in like manner and hence is essentially a hybrid combination of functional, ornamental and formal

2, 3 Hans Hollein, Austrian Travel Bureau, Vienna, 1976-78. Collaged under a neutral arch are a series of conventional signs of travel. The images may be stereotypes, as in Pop Art (perhaps a necessity for a travel bureau), but they are given an overall plot and careful detailing that are anything but clichéd.

incidents. For example, Hans Hollein's Austrian Travel Bureau in Vienna is a compilation of identifiable signs: broken, eroded columns, palm trees and alabaster flags (2,3). On the most primitive level of organisation, such metonymic elements would be laid out haphazardly as in a randomly constructed still life; more developed stages would include a compositional order, a semantic relationship and finally a plot and overall symbolic structure. Within this range of development Hollein's Travel Bureau is somewhere near the top: the parts have some meaning and they tell a modest story. For instance the pyramid falling through the wall signifies travel to Egypt, the eroded column travel to Rome, the palm trees desert, the Mogul dome India, the bird flying in the background air tickets, the life-belt and rails ship tickets and the lead curtain theatre tickets. One pays for all this travel and fantasy at the cashier's desk which is placed, with a certain irony, behind a Rolls Royce radiator grill. Thus a collage of hybrid forms gains meaning through both the metonymic relation of one part to the next and the association of each part with a conventional idea. But what gives the reading momentum is the idea that each element has a role to play in the whole story. Much abstract art – and even randomly collaged realism – lacks momentum and charge.

Although a coherent plot and collection of meaningful elements may be essential to symbolic architecture, we should not assume that the style must always be hybrid. A great deal of traditional architecture integrated symbolism to such an extent that we may fail to notice it. A case in point is Henri Labrouste's Bibliothèque Sainte-Geneviève (1843-50) built opposite the church of Sainte-Geneviève near Notre Dame in Paris (4). For a long time it was admired by Modernists such as Siegfried Giedion for its use of cast iron and sense of space; it is only recently through new readings by Neil Levine and other historians that we have begun to understand it as symbolic architecture. If we consider this building aesthetically, we see an integrated work of repeated arches in the nineteenth-century Neo-Classical style. Large arches to let in light are located above smaller ones in the Early-Renaissance style. We may note the swags and names of famous authors inscribed within the bays, but we would probably not guess that this long, repetitive building tells an interesting story.

As a young student, Labrouste went to Paestum and drew versions of its Greek temples, one of which had a row of columns down the centre. He also drew versions of another temple in which he imagined a decorative programme that memorialised the names of famous Greek warriors whose shields were also displayed as a form of interior ornament. Several years later (1831) Victor Hugo wrote *Notre Dame de Paris,* a novel in which the cathedral itself figures as a major protagonist. He predicted a sad end for symbolic buildings, saying that the new genres of writing – journalism and the novel – would submerge architecture: 'ceci tuera cela'. (One hundred and forty years later Marshall McLuhan made a similar forecast that, in turn, electronic media would kill writing.) The prospect was frightening for an architect.

4, 5 Henri Labrouste, Bibliothèque Sainte-Geneviève, Paris, 1843-50. Integrated symbolism, both understated and esoteric, but carefully worked out and credible nonetheless. Note the way motifs and forms are stylised in the building, which relates to the urban space and to Notre Dame in the distance.

Notre Dame, and other cathedrals, had been for France a type of encyclopedia, a *summa* of knowledge and faith. In the age of newspapers and fast printing it would no longer be necessary for architecture to fulfil this role. Labrouste answered this argument with his building – a *summa* where the world's knowledge is symbolised by writing and the summation of architectural styles.

One enters through an Egyptian hypostyle hall – constructed, surprisingly, from cast-iron girders – and then climbs up to the main reading room which has a row of central columns like the temple Labrouste drew at Paestum. On the exterior, Greek swags unite Roman arches while above, the blind arcades – which are meant to recall the cemeteries of Pisa – are combined with Albertian medallions and nineteenth-century engineering. Interior bookstacks are reflected on the outside by the inscriptions on stone. The names of famous philosophers, writers and scientists are laid out in rows of type, like the newspaper columns which were supposedly to supplant the architectural ones. With this building Labrouste was arguing that architecture had existed as an unbroken thread of significance from Egypt to Greece to Italy to nineteenth-century France. His building says to Notre Dame just down the street and to the church of Sainte-Geneviève opposite that architecture will not be killed by the printing press. And furthermore it says this in a highly detailed, Classical tongue where even the sharp-focus swags have specific meaning (5).

From this and many other examples of Classical and Gothic buildings we may conclude that a symbolic architecture need not have an emphatically hybrid composition, although like Hollein's Travel Bureau it may choose to do so.

ABSTRACT REPRESENTATION

If a symbolic architecture may be hybrid or integrated, it has to steer a very careful path between abstraction and representation. We approach works of art with expectations which direct what we see, as psychologists and theorists such as E. H. Gombrich have shown. These expectations are part of our *Weltanschauung*, or world view, and part of our past aesthetic experience as well as present mood.

As a work of art unfolds before us, we constantly project hypotheses: 'the plot will go this way, the path will lead that way, soon there will be variations of previous themes, and inevitably there will be an ending'. These hypotheses result in part from the structure of human experience, the natural drama of human time with its beginning, middle and end. But the act of hypothesising is also built into the structure of art and its syntax, and the structure of the mind and its concepts. It therefore follows that an architecture which is too abstract will not appeal to what one already knows and believes, while one which is too representational will leave little to the imagination and prevent the autonomous language of architecture from doing its work.

Symbolist poets and painters of the last century understood this as clearly as the Zen aesthetician: to name something is to confine it, while merely to suggest it is to give it added power. The importance of allowing the language of art its inherent expressiveness, its abstract meaning, was a tenet formulated by artists such as Gauguin from the recognition of the power of suggestion. And no doubt the Symbolists were half-right. Suggestive veiling, ambiguity, multiple meanings and the autonomous language of art are powerful devices which must be respected. But as their followers, the Expressionists, demonstrated in an art that became too autonomous and private, the content must return, from time to time, to clearly stated themes. And it matters that these themes are significant and credible to the viewer.

A fundamental problem in symbolic architecture is how to represent these common themes so that they neither conflict with other requirements nor become too blatant – simplistic one-liners. Representational painting can be, and indeed usually is, straightforward about its figuration. Architecture can only occasionally be as representational – for example in a commercial or religious context. Usually it has to be more subtle and understated in its meanings; it has to be a background for other events as well as an object of appreciation in itself.

There are several obvious ways in which architecture can work as both background and foreground. As background, it can use the general coloration and material of its surroundings as does Labrouste's Bibliothèque. Or it can abstract and repeat patterns, as with the windows and cornice motifs of this same building. Abstraction and generalisation have always been key methods in the architect's formal repertoire, but for a symbolic building they are not enough. They have to be combined with iconic motifs, with stylisations and variations of such images. This entails a type of double design, which I can best illustrate with my own work since it is obviously the most familiar to me. I have however written about this abstract representation within the work of other contemporary architects.‡

For nearly every object, or facade, I make a series of nine or ten quick logic studies which immediately show various possibilities: some of these are then successively stylised. This process of investigation is directed towards

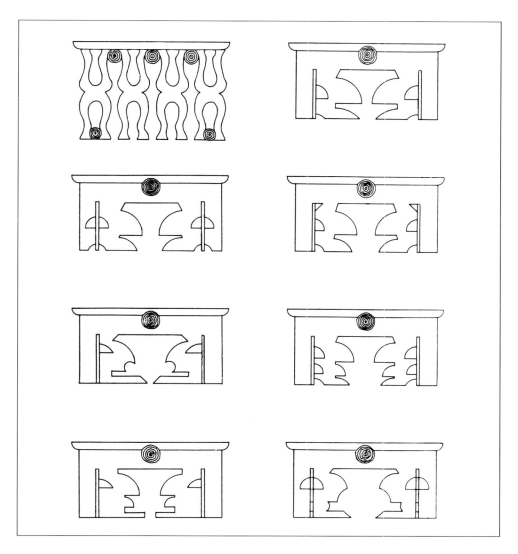

both the functional and the symbolic requirements and the goal is to integrate these two systems into a third, or formal system. I shall use the example of the design of a modest piece – a table to hold magazines and objects – to illustrate this process, as the functions and signs involved are relatively simple (6).

The table was for the California Room of the Elemental House and therefore had to relate to the themes and colours of the room, for instance the light background made up of creams, whites and blues (7-9). It had to signify the primitive beauty of the immediate area (in Rustic Canyon), so I thought of using a heavy log as part of its structure. Since the cross-section of a log is a natural symbol for the sun – with its annual rings and 'rays' – I was rather pleased to discover this redundancy in my choice. The log as sun symbol relates to other solar imagery in the house, and especially to its location within the Ignis Pavilion.

One question was whether to use the log as a bottom or top support, and both solutions were tried. But I had to incorporate other meanings concerned with the table's location within the overall plan. One of the symbolic systems for the Elemental House was based on two of John Milton's poems. The relevant lines for this particular place in the sequence spoke of Jonson's and Shakespeare's plays and even included a reference to the latter's naturalness and rusticity:

6 Quick logic studies of the faces table show some of the variations in structure, and a resolution of four main images.

'Or sweetest Shakespeare, fancy's child,
Warble his native wood-notes wild.'

235

The sectioned log already symbolised the 'wood-notes wild', but I needed the 'warblers', or actors with their masks. Hence the table would have two faces, stylised in profile, to symbolise these actors. Since I didn't want these faces to be too obvious, they were combined with other Californian images: the palm tree (there is one immediately outside), two half-suns and then, between these images, the silhouette of a strawberry. Thus if one follows the stages of design, it is clear how these four basic ideas were abstracted and resolved into a formal balance so that none is too strong and all are suggested. Grimacing actors, palm trees, suns and strawberry are all turned into a workable structure that holds up a log painted light cream to symbolise the sun. This in turn supports a table top painted light blue to symbolise the sky. All of this just to make a small table.

Perhaps this utilitarian object is overdesigned, and it certainly isn't the last word in beauty, but it does illustrate my point about double design. One must abstract the functions *and* the symbolic programmes, stylise both and try to resolve them. If one isn't concerned with both, one runs the risk of falling foul of those opposed twins, functionalism and ornamentalism, which have trapped so many designers. If the architect and interior designer are to produce resonant symbols, they must establish links between these opposite levels of design and not fall back on a type of appliqué or packaging.

There are also perceptual reasons for adopting the dual approach of abstract representation. On the one hand, architecture must be abstract because its own language of structure and rhythm has to be allowed to work as an autonomous expressive system, and also because it has to appeal to a wide audience through generality and typicality. On the other hand, it must also be representational. It must use images that are recognisable, which refer to people's hopes and fears, and portray an appropriate social and spiritual content. These motivations are irreducible and, unfortunately, contradictory. They place opposite demands, forcing the architect to be a social realist one moment and an abstract artist the next. Abstract representation, this strange-sounding conglomerate, is not marginal for symbolic architecture, but its essence.

7, 8   The faces table, 1982. The sectioned log, painted light cream, symbolises the sun with its round shape and annual rings. Its cracks and imperfections, in contrast to the flat finish, denote the rustic context.

9   The faces table in its context with other light forms, sunburst motifs, blues, creams and a painting by Roland Coate, *Baja Sands*.

236

SEEING WITH BELIEVING

At its best symbolic architecture is like successful symbolism in other arts; it provides a condensed sign in which the part stands for the whole, for a much larger area of meaning. A successful symbol, as we've seen in the examples of the Egyptian Temple and Thomas Tresham's Triangular Lodge, can mediate between the everyday and the eternal as an immediate, impacted sign – in the same way that the *petite madeleine* called up for Proust's narrator a whole world of experience. Moreover, the architectural symbol is both immediate and presentational, like a musical theme, and suggestive and explicit, like a religious symbol.

Symbolic architecture, like symbolic art, inevitably demands a particular way of seeing. One can't judge a Vermeer painting or Chartres cathedral within a solely aesthetic framework without missing more than half the point. Symbolic objects demand to be seen through concepts, knowledge and finally beliefs. Other things being equal, the more background knowledge one has of a painting or building the greater one's appreciation of it. This direct correlation between understanding and experience was formulated in the eighteenth century by, among others, the Scottish philosopher Archibald Alison. He asserted that since the experience of beauty was largely in the mind, then the greater the mental associations called up by an object the greater its beauty. Acceptance of this theory obviously leads to the call for more richly associated buildings, and also demands greater learning on the part of the viewer. What are its implications for contemporary society?

The public for art and architecture today is probably becoming increasingly sophisticated and is certainly better educated than at any time in the past, if the number and level of college degrees are anything to go by. The complexity of post-industrial life requires a mental agility, if not a developed taste. This, coupled with increased leisure, travel, further education and what has been referred to as the knowledge explosion – the dissemination of advanced scholarship – has produced the new common reader. He is likely to have an acquaintance with the art of several cultures and a well-stocked bank of visual images and thus would be able to assimilate a breadth of reference in his literature and architecture. It is conceivable that a rich and symbolic art would appeal to him.

Whatever the case in the future, it remains true that we do see through our concepts, even aesthetic ones, and in that sense we see with our mind's eye. Although this faculty may recently have been weakened through disuse, or frustrated by too much utilitarian raw material, it is interesting to note how quickly this mode of perception has been able to re-emerge and become a new norm. Already an appetite for the canons of Post-Modernism is developing in America and Japan, and with every year the taste for the genre is bound to become more demanding and refined. The demands may finally lead to an imperative: the themes must be public and significant. An art which is in-significant, as the root word suggests, is of little value, of no importance, and dismissed after an initial notice. And the concept of 'significant form', if it relies on form alone, does not compensate for a lack of significant content. So the actual themes which art and architecture represent are important in themselves and one of the organising motives for their structure.

In the Thematic House, we have used perennial ideas for organisation and composition – the ideas of time, cultural history, cosmic events and rhythms, anthropomorphism and nature – combined with personal themes. They may not be relevant to everyone and they may not fill the vacuum created by our agnostic age for others, but at the very least they are credible and not immediately contradicted by science. I would even argue that themes such as cultural history are based on 'objective value', but this argument would entail another book much longer than the present one.

In any case, the theme, like the classical *concetto* or art concept, has an artistic function as well as an heuristic one: it unifies disparate parts of a work. It operates essentially as a dynamic power that, like Coleridge's notion of the faculty of the imagination, pulls together heterogeneous elements and diffuses a common spirit throughout. Like the neo-Platonic idea in art the theme may act as an ideal unifying a series of enumerated objects, an archetypal form or a standard to be reached. Symbolic art and architecture project such ideals, just as the perceiver projects ideas onto an object in the form of hypotheses. The ideas, or hypotheses, then limit, unify and collect the impressions received by the senses into a pattern which ultimately challenges the belief of the viewer.

To insist on public and significant themes is not, however, to say that symbolic architecture must be ideological – the potential trap of Platonic aesthetics, as well as the very real problem faced by Platonic politics. The disadvantages of such art, as illustration or propaganda, are too well-known in this century to need elaboration. This kind of work quickly becomes obsolete, or tiring, when its ideology is exhausted. Besides, in an open democracy, any supposedly final system of ideas or values appears implausible, literally incredible – a second reason for rejecting a simple idealism, both aesthetic and political, while still embracing design based on ideas.

The architect and the client have therefore to walk a fine line between ideology and thematic architecture. They have to create and perceive mixed systems of form and content and then make fine discriminations within them, being always attentive to errors of imbalance: 'too much abstraction, too little suggestion, too great an ideology, too little expression' are phrases of degree which mediate between the dialectic of form and meaning. If the architect is not motivated by themes outside architecture he will produce a dull formalism; if he is only motivated by such concerns he will produce a bad building. And even if he avoids both these negatives he won't necessarily produce anything good; but at least there is a greater chance.

‡ See 'Abstract Representation', *Architectural Design* 53, 7/8, 1983 which discusses the work of Michael Graves in this context, pp. 19-22, 101-102.

APPENDIX A
Design Credits for The Elemental House

DESIGN OF PAVILIONS
Charles Jencks, Buzz Yudell

DESIGN OF GARDEN
Maggie Keswick aided by Pamela Burton

GARDEN PLAN
Maggie Keswick

COLOUR CONSULTANT
Tina Beebe

DESIGN OF FURNITURE
Charles Jencks

CALIFORNIA PAINTINGS
Roland Coate

LISE FRAGMENTS SCULPTURE
Robert Graham

WALL RELIEF
Penny Jencks

AER SCULPTURE
Timothy Woodman

WATERCOLOURS OF THE FOUR ELEMENTS
Sidney Hurwitz

AQUA FIGURE AND WAVES
Charles Moore

LETTERING
Charles Jencks

PHOTOGRAPHY
Tim Street-Porter, Charles Jencks (as noted)

WORKING DRAWINGS AND SUPERVISION
Peter Zingg, Moore Ruble Yudell

CONCEPTUAL DRAWINGS
Charles Jencks

SECTIONAL DRAWINGS AND SITE PLAN
Amir Fava

CONSTRUCTION OF MAIN PAVILIONS
Carde Killefer

CONSTRUCTION OF HERMITAGE
Per Christiansen

CONSTRUCTION OF ENTRANCE GATE
David Bemis

Design Credits for The Thematic House

This house has taken many years to design and there have been many designers involved with it. Working out the exact design credits would be a difficult affair, especially since part of the design was collaborative, and intentionally so. In general however, the design was under my control – which is not to say that I thought up all the ideas. Rather, I always tried to integrate the different ideas and themes through drawings – plans, perspectives, axonometrics, elevations – and written programmes. By and large, the shell working drawings and specifications were controlled by the Terry Farrell Partnership; the kitchen working drawings and specifications by Johnny Grey Associates; the jacuzzi drawings, and indeed major idea, by Piers Gough.

BRIEF HISTORY OF THE MICHAEL FISHER COLLABORATION JUNE-OCTOBER 1978

The house was bought in May 1978. Its previous owner, an elderly woman, had done only basic maintenance for many years. Some original features and parts of mouldings had disappeared, and the studio was not connected to the main house. In June, at the recommendation of Nicky Johnson, Maggie and I went to Michael Fisher of Fisher Associates with the idea that we would design the house and he would detail and carry out our plans.

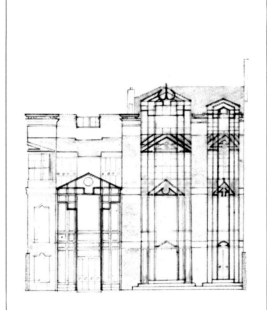

We started with two basic ideas: that the building's street facade should be related to its context – thus drawings of the grammar of 'rabbit' balusters, chimney shapes, dormer windows etc. are described as 'local motifs' on the drawing sketch (1) – and that we should make use of double-height spaces, arcades to the garden and a sequence of stairs and terraces. The top, flat roof was to have solar collectors with our initials – M and C – and other signs echoed in the balustrades. The original design foresaw a 'Terrace House' which would combine the typical London terrace with our idea of three or four terraces spilling down to the garden. Next, we generated alternatives which provided for an extension over the existing garage, the re-use of 'rabbit' rails and the extension of the cornice lines. All these features have been realised, although the addition is only half the height shown here and completed with a curved roof.

Face motifs (Jencksiana) and open planning (flowing space with vistas, often punched through double height) predominate in these sketches. Moving the stair to the centre of the house was an idea both Terry Farrell and Maggie had independently. The idea of having two or more conservatories running up the back of the facade to integrate it visually was worked out and united with the underlying ABBA rhythm of the house. My initial elevations show an attempt to integrate and contrast two different grammars – glass verticals and masonry horizontals. Many of the drawings show an attempt to reinforce this dualism with demi-forms in plans – the idea of Classical forms incompleted, or juxtaposed (2). All these schemes allowed for some direct access to the garden, usually from the side. The major zoning of the house's space shown here was retained, except for the Foursquare Room, which changed places with the Architectural Library.

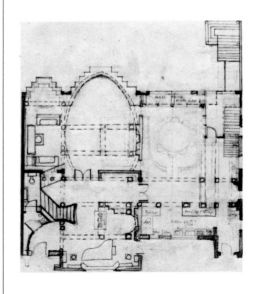

However, by October, with the rough design clear and the house laid out, it became obvious that Michael Fisher's office wasn't large enough to carry through all these increasingly complex intentions.

TERRY FARRELL PARTNERSHIP NOVEMBER 1978 – CIRCA MARCH 1982

We discussed who might help us, and Maggie mentioned Terry Farrell. I thought that this was a good idea because, having heard him lecture twice (at the AA and RIBA Conferences),

I knew him to be flexible and interested in collaborating with others. In addition, I thought his technical expertise and building experience would compensate for our weakness in those areas. I showed him my drawings and mentioned that we wanted to design as a group with him. Specifically, I asked if I could use his office, or a draughtsman in it, and he kindly agreed – a situation that worked for the next three years (with David Quigley, Simon Sturgis and Richard Soloman). I gave him a copy of *The Language of Post-Modern Architecture* and spelled out my Post-Modernist intentions, which were mostly symbolic. At that time Farrell's work (with Nicholas Grimshaw) was Late-Modern and High-Tech, but he was definitely veering away from his partner.

Terry had the ingenious idea of splitting the building programme into two parallel areas, with the Hodgson Brothers working on the shell and Jack Gilbert and other carpenters on the internal fittings and details. The time frame suggested that the house would be largely finished by June 1979. In the event, this was naive, but the parallel management was conceptually very wise for it allowed the separation of fast and slow, and big and small work.

Terry, David, Maggie and I met for design sessions once every two weeks or so in January. In the beginning these sessions were fruitful collaborations, even if time-consuming and unbalanced (as both client and designer I had a preponderant edge on the discussions). The resulting joint design had a central stair designed by me, then modified by Terry. Terry also suggested that planning permission for the addition of a full storey would be impossible to get and introduced a half-level addition (the Architectural Library). On the garden facade, we attempted to merge the Jencksiana with vertical conservatories. Terry, together with his heating consultant Ralph Lebens, modified our conservatory designs. Where Maggie and I had proposed a solar panel scheme, they suggested passive solar glazing with square bays, a central 'plenum' heat-store and circulation up the Solar Stair. This stair was in fact not clarified until about December. Once we had decided to put it in the centre of the house, I exaggerated the treads as sunburst motifs of a curvilinear or flamboyant kind. Working with clay models, I designed the treads and risers so that they would appear from below as sunrays (this after Maggie and I looked at the sunray staircase in Inigo Jones' Queen's House in Greenwich). David Quigley then realised that the house had fifty-two steps – one for each week in the year – so we added seven vertical divisions for the days. Where there were no reinforcing bars in the cylinder of the stairs, we tried to open vistas: several of my plans show the penetration of the stair into the study and kitchen, which is now only visual. Terry Farrell and David French understood how this stair could hold up both itself and the two adjacent chimneys.

We made further clarifications in December to the dormers, the gable and the elevation (where I introduced a split chimney with a Jencksiana above it in place of the single chimney). Terry clarified the plans and their relation to the stair. I designed the garden elevation with Jencksiana and Terry proposed 'steel-framed frames' (the keystone and two steel Jencksianas is the result). We clarified the library and I proposed the Hildebrandtian S-curve for the roof after Terry said it wouldn't cost appreciably more.

By January, we had advanced considerably. Maggie had proposed a two-tiered garden with a central plot and had thought of lowering the living room conservatory (now the Sun Dial Arcade) towards it. Terry had invented the study galleries above the kitchen/dining room and had thought of sneaking the main dressing room and bathroom into the two half-levels. We all worked on the kitchen layout until it took on a U-shaped configuration. We then further articulated the stair and agreed on the concept of an alternating ABBA rhythm across the front and back elevations. Thus by January 1979 all the major features had been designed except for the jacuzzi, master bedroom, little top floor kitchen and downstairs flat. Even the London column had been designed as a symbolic bookcase column – something that influenced Terry in the design of his office columns. We were in America from January 10th-April 1st and so the design phase slowed down, but preliminary clearing and demolition was started. A certain autonomy was granted David Quigley and he soon implanted ornamental brickwork that became known as 'Quigleyisms' (of which two faces remain in the basement). David French, the structural engineer, worked with Terry Farrell both on the stair and study designs and their combined expertise allowed the ideas to be realised. For the next few years the design and building progressed in a chicken and egg manner and it is easier to discuss it area by area than in terms of a sequence.

ELEVATIONS The three main elevations neared a stage of final design in the Summer of 1980. By then I had established three main principles:
1   The garden facade should contain the faces of the children and parents, with transformations of them on the other two sides. These would form vertical white figures against a brick background and integrate the downspouts into the design wherever possible.

2   Existing vocabulary such as 'rabbits' should be used but in a transformed way. The 'window' as a decorative theme developed into the grid square.

3   The London columns should be a unifying theme for the side elevation. For this, I designed a five-part elevation of columns with V-shaped voids reminiscent of the London sun bursting through the clouds (cf. the London column in *AD*, 5/1980 Post-Modern Classicism (3). By March 1980, I had in fact formulated Post-Modern Classicism as a concept and was thinking about its style as an ordering principle for the house.)

From my sketch of five columns Terry Farrell and Simon Sturgis built a model of the side elevation and library and designed the structure of the roof so that it ended in a nice ogee overlooking the garden. From their model and drawings I then developed the three facades as an integral unity (see the coloured elevations). I sent the drawings down from Scotland in July with a note to Terry specifying the problems, which occurred mostly on the garden facade: the skeletal 'faces' were too busy, the stairs wouldn't integrate with the study balcony (they were later dropped), and the steel and glass conservatories didn't meet the ground any better than they met the sky.

We met soon after to clarify some of this, and Joe Foges (who had taken over from David Quigley) suggested that the conservatory windows should be giant casements, since we were aiming for a London vernacular. Terry suggested the lifting mechanism used for theatre fire-curtains and thus we had a new idea. Later that Summer, I sent Simon quick logic solutions for the conservatory and jacuzzi keystone. One of these was adopted; it had a head, shoulders (flare), two arms, a belt and two legs – all disguised in the window form (4). The axonometric of the house that I produced in Scotland had related the back garden to the terraces on the side and study, and shown all the facades and London columns in a unified Post-Modern Classical style. Later on, certain elements were further simplified, for instance the side London columns were dropped and the garden stairway – which Simon and I designed with the Steelways manufacturer – was integrated with the garden terrace. The side and front elevations were mostly designed by me after twenty or thirty sketch attempts. These show, on the street facade, a symmetry of doors (one false), the transformation of the rabbit motif and the Hildebrandtian curve ending in a crown – later a grid. Initially, this grid was surmounted by palm fronds, but we soon realised this was inadequate and I started a long discussion with my sister Penny on the design of two sculptures – personifications of Art and Architecture – to replace them. These were eventually dropped, at Maggie's suggestion, as being too assertive on an already complex facade, and new vases are contemplated. But the side elevation designs had shown that, visually and symbolically, two focal points were needed as the culmination to the two uprising curves – even if this proved to be urbanistically provocative.

MOONWELL   I had conceived the Moonwell as a 'column' of space capped by a flaring capital and surfaced with mirror. Maggie saw the point of increasing the horizontal span of the mirror and Terry pointed out the asymmetry of the top roofline. We modified the arch shapes to be repetitive, and Simon designed these throughout. Ilinca Cantacuzino and I designed the moon on the mirror as the culmination of the 'facade' (which was a transformation of the conservatory facades). The story it tells is that of Liu Hai and the three-legged toad, a Chinese myth which had amused John Keswick (who had a great collection of three-legged toads).

DOME OF WATER   Simon Sturgis and I determined that the jacuzzi should be oval-shaped and we gave this, as a problem, to Piers Gough. He had the brilliant idea of turning the Jencksiana upside down to form a dome over the jacuzzi. He and I then looked at Baroque oval domes and his *trompe l'oeil* design combines elements of Borromini's S. Carlo alle Quattro Fontane with elements from other Baroque churches. His 'ground' (over the head) was then made as a mixture of De Stijl cubiforms and Lutyens' stripes (Maggie's idea). I was worried about the possible sacrilege of this inversion, but a programme on a British Orphic villa (with a similar plan centring on a sun motif) convinced me that the precedents were sacred in general, and therefore acceptable. Ilinca Cantacuzino and I worked through about twenty versions of the seasons, and finally a set was engraved on the glass lights.

SOLAR STAIR AND STAIR RAIL   I designed the stair rail after many sketches and discussions with various manufacturers, including Steelways, and finally Colin Sullivan of Lewis Design (Spiral Stairways). The stainless steel rails were cheaper than other types and high credit for the exacting workmanship must go to Sullivan and his crew. (The stair has a very tight radius, which is why two companies turned the job down immediately.) The sun, earth and moon flowing around the centre in a spiral suggested to me the whirlpool galaxies. After some cosmological study, I wrote a programme for Eduardo Paolozzi's *The Black Hole* mosaic. He and I traded books and ideas, as well as sketches, and this resulted in one of the more successful collaborations. Ilinca Cantacuzino and I did about six versions of the signs of the zodiac until they were sufficiently abstract to be part of the architecture. It was during

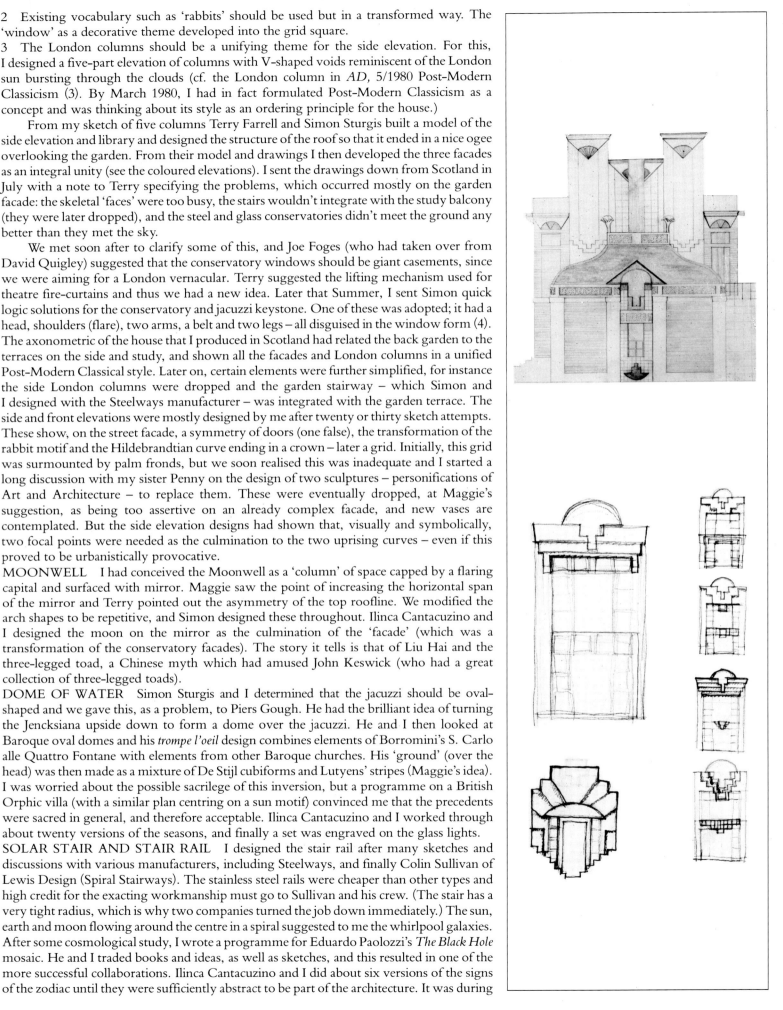

this time (while in America) that I became aware of the philosophy (or mode) of abstract representation: the necessity for the designer to abstract representational themes to a level of generality so that they can be repeated and mass-produced.

TOP FLOOR INTERIORS   After the exterior facades, I worked on the interior iconography and designs for Lily, Johnny and Nan's rooms. Valentine Abbott and I did the window shade designs, Maggie did the lily flowers on the bed and the bed design, while I designed most of the cabinets, shelves and other built-in furniture – beds, doors, doorknobs, sunbursts, moon lights, globes and surrounds (in the Moonwell) etc. Mark Lewis of Johnny Grey Associates laid out Nan's kitchen and followed our basic iconographic intentions.

ARCHITECTURAL LIBRARY   I designed the furniture, bookhouses (representing the history of architecture), sunburst ceiling (except for David Quigley's contribution of the split rays), doors, slide/windows and lights (with Molly Rubenstein of Erco). Simon and Terry saw that older windows from the house were re-used around the terrace off the library.

MAGGIE'S STUDY   I designed the false stepped window and we all designed the stepped window it was imitating. I designed the mouldings and door, Maggie the moving shelves, and Steve Agombar worked out the mirror design.

MASTER BEDROOM   I designed almost all of the interior foursquare elements except the mechanism for the sinking/rising TV, which was devised by Steve Agombar and John Longhurst.

BATHPOOL   Maggie designed the mirrors, staggers and the wide stairs incorporating the loo, and I insisted on the mid-level water line. We worked on the special tiles with Jay Bonner, and I designed the stencil of water/ducks with Maggie's help.

STUDY BATHROOM AND LOO   Maggie designed the furniture, I did the doorknobs, mouldings and shower.

LIVING ROOMS   I designed most of the elements such as the window/door system and furniture, but Michael Graves designed the Winter and Spring fireplaces according to a programme I had written. Celia Scott sculpted Eduardo Paolozzi as Hephaestus (Winter) and Penny Jencks sculpted Cressida Hare, Florence Phillips and Marcia Hare as April, May and June. 'Egypt' was to have been designed by Bob Stern, but in the event he never met our deadlines and so I had to do it.

COSMIC OVAL   I designed the oval and built it with Steve Agombar and John Longhurst. The complex programme for the space has been written but not yet fully realised. Consultants include Dr McNally (Royal Observatory), Robert van Pelt (an expert on the cosmology of previous cultures) and the artist William Stok. Together with Maggie we determined the figures representing open-mindedness, travel, eclecticism and creativity.

KITCHEN   The kitchen was developed by Maggie, myself, Terry and Simon. Then after various consultations with kitchen specialists, Maggie hired Johnny Grey Associates. I did the perspective sketches, detailed decorative plans, Hindu orders, 'spoonglyph' and window decoration, while Johnny did the working drawings for Indian Summer and Mark Lewis the drawings for Autumn. After this, it was painted by Paul and Janet Czainski, Pierre Beaudry, Sheila Sartin, Valentine Abbott and several other painters including Edgar Sirs. Adrian Everitt developed my sketches for the iconography.

COSMIC LOO   I did the decoration and iconography which were then interpreted by Steve Agombar and John Longhurst.

BASEMENT FLAT   The layout was by Terry, Simon and Maggie, and the design of kitchen front by Terry, Simon and myself. The internal kitchen fittings were by Mark Lewis; the conservatory idea was Terry's, the elevations mine.

HEATING SYSTEM   Originally the solar aspect was confined to panels, but Terry and Ralph Lebens thought up the idea of a passive solar glass wall. Underfloor storage was installed in the basement but later blocked up after the size of the conservatories was reduced.

GARDEN   The garden was designed mostly by Maggie although I designed the brick and paving layout and the trellis/window/door sequence representing the twelve months of the year. We are consulting Ian Hamilton Finlay on further iconography.

SUNDIAL ARCADE   Worked out in detail and designed by Mark Lennox-Boyd; seats and terraces designed by me.

This list is not exhaustive, but it allows the major points to be made: Maggie did much of the functional thinking at the start; I did most of the visual and iconographic design, including all the furniture; Terry Farrell provided the essential back-up team and a number of key suggestions; Steve Agombar and John Longhurst did very good interpretative carpentry, especially while we were away; and many artists worked with us on the programmes.

Photographic Credits

INTRODUCTION
Photograph by Richard Bryant

CHAPTER I
All photographs by Charles Jencks except: Contemporary photograph (25); Caroline Courtauld (2); Maggie Keswick (15-17); Kipp (4); John Portman Associates (1); Joseph Rykwert (3, 5-6)

CHAPTER II
All photographs by Charles Jencks except: Morse Collection, New York (2)

CHAPTER III
All photographs by Charles Jencks except: Tim Street-Porter (1, 3, 7, 9, 12, 14-15, 17a-17b, 19, 25-26, 29, 34)

CHAPTER IV
All photographs by Charles Jencks

CHAPTER V
All photographs by Richard Bryant except: Contemporary photograph 96-97 (2); By Gracious Permission of Her Majesty the Queen 192-193 (3); Charles Jencks 88-89 (2), 90-91 (3, 7), 92-93 (10, 12), 100-101 (1-3, 5), 104-105 (2), 110-111 (2), 114-115 (1), 116-117 (2), 118-119 (2-3), 126-127 (4), 132-133 (3), 136-137 (3), 138-139 (2), 144-145 (3-4), 146-147 (2-5), 150-151 (3), 158-159 (1-2), 164-165 (3), 166-167 (2-5), 178-179 (1-5), 180-181 (1-2), 182-183 (2), 190-191 (1-2), 192-193 (4), 196-197 (2), 198-199 (2), 204-205 (1), 210-211 (5), 214-215 (4-5), 218-219 (4-7), 220-221 (1-2); Ianthe Ruthven 90-91 (4-5), 140-141 (2), 156-157 (1), 164-165 (4), 194-195, 196-197 (1), 202-203 (3), 208-209 (1), 212-213 (1); The Netherlands Office of Fine Art 124-125 (2), Trustees, The National Gallery, London 90-91 (6), 180-181 (3); Trustees, The Wallace Collection, London 148-149 (4)

CHAPTER VI
All photographs by Charles Jencks except: Frumkin Gallery, New York (1)